S. Prakash Sethi and Dow Votaw, *editors*

THE PRENTICE-HALL SERIES
IN ECONOMIC INSTITUTIONS AND SOCIAL SYSTEMS

Marketing,
Society,
and Conflict

Marketing, Society, and Conflict

Sidney J. Levy
Northwestern University

Gerald Zaltman
University of Pittsburgh

PRENTICE-HALL, INC., *Englewood Cliffs, New Jersey*

Library of Congress Cataloging in Publication Data

Levy, Sidney J
  Marketing, society, and conflict.

  (Prentice-Hall series in economic institutions and
social systems)
  Includes bibliographical references.
    1. Marketing.   2. Marketing—Social aspects.
3. Social change.   I. Zaltman, Gerald, joint author.
II. title
HF5415.L4843   301.5'1   74-34224
ISBN 0-13-557819-1
ISBN 0-13-557801-9 pbk.

Printed in the United States of America

10 9 8 7 6 5 4 3 2 1

PRENTICE-HALL INTERNATIONAL, Inc., *London*
PRENTICE-HALL OF AUSTRALIA, Pty. Ltd., *Sydney*
PRENTICE-HALL OF CANADA, Ltd., *Toronto*
PRENTICE-HALL OF INDIA PRIVATE LIMITED, *New Delhi*
PRENTICE-HALL OF JAPAN, Inc., *Tokyo*

To
RICHARD M. CLEWETT
friend and colleague

Contents

ix

Foreword

After having been a part of the curriculum in many schools of business for twenty years or more, the field now vaguely described as "business and society" seems at last to be coming into focus. A common core of interest has begun to evolve and to give promise of providing the integrating concepts of teaching and research that have been so conspicuous by their absence in the past. Evidence of this long delayed crystallization can be found in new course descriptions and outlines, in the research interests of those working in the field, and in the proceedings of conferences convened for the purpose of examining the proper content and parameters of this important area of practical, as well as academic, concern. The field and its integrating theme appear very clearly, as suggested above, to be the complex, dynamic, two-way relationship between the economic institutions of our society, with which most schools of business are primarily concerned, and the social systems in which those institutions now operate and are likely to operate in the future.

It would be incorrect and misleading to suggest that the interaction between business and society has not been a part of the business school curriculum in the past. In one form or another, this interaction has played an important role in business and society courses for many years. There are, however, several basic differences between what has been done in the past and the new rallying point we now see evolving. The old, and still dominant, approach has been very narrow in its emphasis and in its boundaries and has all too often been limited to little more than an instructor's own specialty in such areas as social control, business and government, or antitrust. Even where an instructor's narrow predispositions are not present, the "social" side of the relationship is often viewed as being static, or relatively so, and external to the current decision or situational context; and the primary goals of the course are those of explaining the phenomenon of business to the students and of analyzing the requirements of business-like, efficient, or responsible behavior in a rather loose social sense. Furthermore, the emphasis is almost wholly the private, large, and industrial aspects of the economic sector, with little, if any, attention devoted to the public, small, or nonindustrial variables.

The flaws in this approach are obvious, and changes are already beginning to take place. What appears to be evolving, and what we believe should be evolving, is a much greater interest in the dynamics of the whole system. What is needed is a systematic analysis of the effects (noneconomic as well as economic) of business on other institutions and on the social system, and of the effects of changes in other institutions and in the social system on the economic sector. Most important, perhaps, the stage should be set for an understanding of the basic assumptions, attitudes, values, concepts, and ideologies that underlie a particular arrangement of economic institutions and social systems and of how changes in these assumptions affect the arrangements and the interactions among the various parts of the whole system.

Two other points ought also to be made here. *First,* although most schools of business do not behave as though it were so, they are actually engaged in training the managers of tomorrow and not the managers of today. As the relationships between economic institutions and their social environment become more intimate and as each part of the whole system becomes more sensitive and more responsive to changes in the other parts, how much more important it is going to be for the manager to understand the dynamics of the system as a whole than it is for him to know what the momentary conformation happened to be when he was in school. It seems to us, further, that one of the manifestations of an industrially mature society will be the economic sector's diminishing importance and, as a consequence, a reversal of the flow of influence from the economic sector to society as a whole. The manager of the future will need to be more sensitive to changes in society than he ever was in the past. His training will have to include a very different congeries of tools and ingredients than it now does.

Second, we think note should be taken of some evidence now beginning to accumulate that suggests that in the future schools of business may come to play the same sort of influential role in the profession of management that schools of law and medicine now play in theirs. If this change should come about, it will become ever more important that managers, during their period of formal education, be provided with those conceptual and analytical tools that best meet the needs of their profession and of the society as a whole. If present forecasts prove to be accurate and "continuing education" becomes a much more important aspect of higher education than it is now, among the first academic institutions to be profoundly affected will be the schools of business. The influence of the schools upon the profession of management will become more immediate and the need for pragmatic training in the interactions between economic institutions and social systems greatly enhanced.

While there is no great disagreement on these general issues, it would be a mistake to assume that there is consensus on the details. We believe that this series takes into account both the agreement on some of the broader points and the lack of consensus on many of the more specific aspects of the changes taking place in the environmental field. For example, there are people who believe that comments like those made above dictate the integration of social materials in all parts of the business curriculum rather than their use in specialized courses devoted to the field; there are many who feel that the bulk of such work should be done in specialized courses; there are many views in the area between these two extremes. We feel that this series is designed in such a way that it can cater to business school curricula of all varieties.

We visualize this series evolving in a set of concentric circles starting at the core and expanding outward. The innermost circle consists of those books that provide much of the basic material that is usually included in the introductory courses in "business and society," including the institutional role of large corporations; government interaction with business; business ideology and values; methodological approaches to measuring the social impact of business activities; corporations and political activities; and the influence of corporate management on the formulation of public policy.

The next circle is made up of books that deal with the impact of corporate activities in specific functional areas. The issues covered here include marketing and social conflict; accounting, accountability, and the public interest; corporate personnel policies and individual rights; and computers and invasion of privacy.

The outermost circle consists of books that are either interdisciplinary or cross-cultural in nature or both. Here we are concerned with the synergistic effect of various economic activities on the society as a whole. On one dimension we are concerned with issues such as how technology gets introduced into society; the economic effects of various types of social welfare programs; how various social activities like health, sanitation, mass transit, and public education are affected by the actions of business; and the social consequences of zero economic growth or population growth. On another level, studies will include comparison between corporate behavior in different social systems.

The concentric circles are not intended to be mutually exclusive, nor do they reflect a certain order of priority in the nature of problems or publication schedule. They are simply a convenient arrangement for thinking about the relationships among various problem areas.

In addition to their role as part of the training provided by collegiate schools of business and management and other social science disciplines, most of the volumes in this series are also of use and interest to managers and to the general public. The basic purpose of the series is to help provide a better understanding of the relationship between our economic institutions and the broader social system, and it is obvious that the need which the series hopes to satisfy is not confined to students of business and management or for that matter even to students. The ultimate goal, we suppose, is not just better corporate social policy but better public policy as well, in the formation of which all citizens participate. Consequently, we have urged the authors of these volumes to keep in mind the broad, in addition to the narrow, targets and to couch their work in language, content, and style that meet both kinds of requirements.

S. Prakash Sethi
Dow Votaw

University of California
Berkeley, California

Prologue

Recent articles in the *Journal of Marketing* highlight various problems in the conceptualization of the field of marketing. David Luck expresses his own confusion with the transitional state of definitions of marketing and social marketing.[1] Similarly, Robert Bartels examines "the identity crisis in marketing" to see the consequences, both beneficial and adverse, of the broadened view of marketing.[2] Luck calls for action by an authoritative body to settle matters, "to forge the definitive statements"; whereas Bartels thoughtfully notes the historical evolution of the scope of marketing, to clarify something of the needs and directions at work. Somewhat amusingly, in illustration of the variety of intellectual currents at work, Bartels notes as one disadvantage to broadening the concept of marketing that the literature has become increasingly esoteric, abstract, and unintelligible to many business practitioners. Although this is no doubt true, as described in Beverlee Anderson's laudatory review of *Metatheory and Consumer Research*,[3] the same issue of the *Journal* nevertheless includes an article by a business practitioner who, asserting that "not all businessmen are myopic," seeks to build on what he refers to as "seminal papers" in the marketing literature.[4] It is a little refreshing when academicians can produce seminal papers for the practitioner community that at the same time confuse some of their academic colleagues.

[1] David J. Luck, "Social Marketing: Confusion Compounded," *Journal of Marketing*, Vol. 38, No. 4, October 1974, pp. 70-72.

[2] Robert Bartels, "The Identity Crisis in Marketing," *Journal of Marketing*, Vol. 38, No. 4, October 1974, pp. 73-76.

[3] Beverlee Anderson, "Review of *Metatheory and Consumer Research*," *Journal of Marketing*, Vol. 38, No. 4, October 1974, pp. 116-17. The book reviewed is Gerald Zaltman, Christian R. A. Pinson, and Reinhard Angelmar, *Metatheory and Consumer Research* (New York: Holt, Rinehart & Winston, Inc., 1973).

[4] Andrew Takas, "Societal Marketing: A Businessman's Perspective," *Journal of Marketing*, Vol, 38, No. 4, October 1974, pp. 2-7.

It is evident that the situation will be nicely stirred should Luck's wish for a special commission of the American Marketing Association come true, but it will not be resolved. Theorists, educators, and practitioners will continue to discuss, debate, write articles, do research, and apply their ideas with various emphases, overlaps, distortions, misunderstandings, and definitions flourishing or waning.

As Bartels notes, the issue is conceptual and debatable. It is also a matter of perspective. Both Luck and Bartels seem to suggest that greater clarity of definition would lead to some resolution of the controversy, with the implication that then people would know their place and not intrude on others' domains. Perhaps so, but not likely. The question is not really one of whether or not the so-called marketers should stick to problems of economic and physical distribution and leave political campaigns, religious evangelism, family planning, or Red Cross solicitation to specialists or to social scientists in general, because marketers *qua* marketers have no right to those problems. It is not a question of Caesar versus God.

The present volume rejects the either-or approach and recognizes that any phenomenon can be thought about, worked on—in theory or in practice—by various disciplines simultaneously. What makes sex political and politics sexual is the determined attention, analysis, and actions of feminists. To dismiss this as a "feminist supremacy syndrome" (à la Luck's reference to those "with a sort of marketing supremacy syndrome") seems pointless and ostrich-like. Because the interest charged for borrowing (or "buying") money is a topic in the field of "finance" does not therefore exclude it from the domain of the marketer, any more than it can be excluded from the domain of the church that condemns it as usury. Economic transactions are spiritual matters (as well as political matters, social matters, aesthetic matters, and so forth), and all those matters can be conceptualized, analyzed, and dealt with practically by marketers as marketing matters.

Basic themes put forth in this volume are these:

1. Attitudes toward marketing are ambivalent. This fact is one of the manifestations of the conflictual character of marketing in general.
2. The ambivalent attitudes toward marketing are intensified by the growth in marketing activity.
3. By radical definition, marketing is the core dynamic mechanism of the social system.
4. Marketing processes in the conventional sense constitute social systems.
5. Social systems such as the family, firm, and so forth are marketing phenomena.
6. Marketing, whether viewed from a narrow or conventional perspective or from a broader perspective, is both a cause and consequence of social change.

7. Social change involves conflict.
8. Conflict in marketing is inherent to the many psychological, social, and economic forces that interact to comprise the total marketing system.
9. Marketing conflict is the expression of contending personal and social values and social changes.
10. Marketing harmony is the expression of social values and social changes that are consonant or compatible.
11. Conflict in marketing can be healthy and desirable.
12. Conventional marketing has developed a set of analytical concepts and tools relevant to nonconventional marketing situations in all social sectors of all societies.
13. Marketers practice conflict management skills.

These ideas will be asserted, analyzed, and illustrated. Relationships between marketing, social values, and conflict will be discussed with special emphasis given to contemporary cases. This introduction is intended to provide a summary orientation, an awareness of the total argument to be developed in this volume.

Somewhat paradoxically, although the great leaps in innovation, technological growth, product synthesis, green revolutions, and so forth, make marketing activities more essential than ever, they also bring with them an intensification of the stigmas that are attached to the idea of marketing. There is considerable ambivalence about marketing. Marketing methods are responded to, and they are disparaged, as are the people who engage in marketing and foster it. Vigorous marketers, whether buyers or sellers, are especially liable to criticism. It seems evident that marketing is both attractive and repellent, suggesting a fascination that requires analysis. Central to the analysis in this volume is the concept of conflict. The thesis is that marketing conflict is intrinsic or inherent in diverse individual and social aims. Marketing conflict is seen as the expression of conflict in economic and social values as well as psychological impulses, acting in a dynamic and essential fashion. Conflict is richly ramified, goes on at many levels, and takes many forms. It is not necessarily destructive, and it is important to study the means by which amelioration, consensus, and resolution come about. Indeed, conflict may be very constructive and purposefully created without necessarily harming individuals or their organizations.

HISTORICAL REVIEW

Bartels provides a main resource delineating modern marketing history from 1900 to the 1960s as a process moving from discovery, conceptualization, and development to reappraisal and reconception. The traditional phases in marketing history described by Bartels will be covered briefly and a closer look will be taken at the emerging marketing themes of the 1970s.

Compared to other disciplines, there is a paucity of marketing theory. There is much superficiality as well as uncertainty about the role and nature of marketing theory. This is evidenced in many of the works published in recent years, although some few individuals, e.g., Gerald Zaltman, Christian Pinson, Reinhard Angelmar, Robert Bartels, and Shelby Hunt, are striving to redress this problem. The shift in relative emphasis from production orientation to consumer orientation was a milestone in marketing history. This shift, termed "the marketing concept," provided a rationale for a new emphasis on marketing activities as distinguished from merely "selling." Supposedly signaling a turn away from aggressive determination to "force" customers to buy goods because they had been produced and needed to be sold, and toward a harmonious and mutually advantageous relationship in which the goods produced were those consumers needed and wanted, the marketing literature exhorted marketers to do marketing research, to "satisfy needs," to "think customer," and so on. This literature produced a struggle between reality and philosophy, as many companies gave lip service to these new ideas in marketing but persisted in their usual practices.

As will be noted later, it is ironic that much of the activity that sprang up as part of the alleged marketing concept—marketing research, advertising aimed at market segmentation and differentiation, recognition of consumers' emotional needs—and thus supposedly promoting a less coercive relationship between sellers and buyers, may be seen as directly involved in the recent conflicting interactions of the modern marketplace falling under the heading of consumerism.

As the category of marketing expands, inputs come from many directions, and more and more groups are becoming involved in conducting marketing and reacting to it. Diverse views develop from the different vantage points of businessmen, ancillary organizations, nonprofit marketing, academic disciplines, consumer advocates, government agencies, publics, and so on. An orchestration of these diverse views is beginning to appear on the horizon.

MARKETING AS A SOCIAL SYSTEM

Among the various inputs, the contributions of the behavioral sciences have been notable. It may be argued that marketing is a pervasive human activity that is therefore amenable to social scientific study as are other human activities. Or it may be argued that marketing is "merely" an applied behavioral science. In either event, there is classical precedent for studying economic institutions as social systems (e.g., Malinowski's great treatise on the *Kula*). The psychologically-oriented analysis called *motivation research*[5]

[5] Sidney J. Levy, "Motivation Research," *Community Organization 1958* (New York: Columbia University Press, 1958), pp. 125-29.

highlighted the human significance of the marketing system. Recent developments in marketing research highlight this.[6]

Major efforts at modeling and at introducing behavioral science have been focused on consumers with the ultimate aim of predicting their actions in the marketplace. Earlier efforts were primarily demographic in character, observing segmentation of markets according to various types of census data. Gradually, especially since 1946, richer and more elaborate analysis took place, drawing on anthropological, sociological, and psychological sources for theory, methods, personnel, vocabulary, and specific variables.[7]

With the development of a behavioral science perspective in marketing, there came a more encompassing perspective that saw the marketing function as highly ramified. Major elements also include the newer view of marketing that stresses the exchange process that identifies marketing tasks in all organizations and examines the special character of marketing in traditional/commercial settings, in social marketing, and in other settings.

A RADICAL VIEW OF MARKETING

Not long ago the role of marketing was defined as: "to move goods and the title to them from manufacturers, farmers, mine operators, and others who create them to consumers. . . . Marketing—which is often referred to as 'distribution' by businessmen—includes all the activities necessary to place tangible goods in the hands of household consumers and industrial users. . . ."[8] More recent literature refers to marketing in broad terms as "emerging discipline of marketing—multifaceted, complex, expanding."[9]

The work of Kotler, Zaltman, and Levy has pressed toward emphasis on the fundamental character of marketing in business and other contexts, seeing its root character in the nature of exchange. All human interactions are then potentially susceptible to a marketing analysis, so that in addition to the transactions included in traditional commercial marketing, there is the possibility of social marketing, and the marketing of organizations, persons, and places. From mass marketing phenomena to what may be termed *intimate marketing* in private dyadic relations, elements basic to giving and getting are at work.

Kotler approaches this with this definition: "Marketing is the set of

[6] Gerald Zaltman and Philip C. Burger, *Marketing Research: Fundamentals and Dynamics* (Hinsdale, Ill.: Dryden Press, 1975).

[7] Gerald Zaltman, *Marketing: Contributions from the Behavioral Sciences* (New York: Harcourt Brace Jovanovich, Inc., 1965).

[8] Charles F. Phillips and Delbert J. Duncan, *Marketing Principles and Methods* (Homewood, Ill.: Richard D. Irwin, 1960), p. 3.

[9] Robert F. Hartley, *Marketing: Management and Social Change* (International Educational Publishers, 1972), p. xi.

human activities directed at facilitating and consummating." More broadly, marketing is the process in which exchanges occur among persons and social groups. The central thesis of this volume is that this process is a dynamic one in which miscellaneous forces interact in ways that participants or observers may evaluate either positively or negatively. The marketing events may be facilitated or hampered, consummated or destroyed, depending on one's view; one man's destruction may be another's consummation.

As Schumpeter points out in his discussion of the circular flow of economic life: "the products of all individuals form a heap somewhere at the end of the economic period, which is then distributed according to certain principles. . . . We can then say that each individual throws a contribution into this great social reservoir, and later receives something from it. To each contribution there corresponds somewhere in the system a claim of another individual; the share of everyone lies ready somewhere."[10] Marketing is the means of working out of this economic abstraction, which refers to the accumulation of individual instances of exchanges. The social product may be composed not only of goods, services, labor, and land, but any elements regarded as having value—time, energy, attention, emotion; all events, even those traditionally defined as "noneconomic," may be interpreted from an economic and marketing point of view.

A discussion of marketing as a cause and consequence of social change is also introduced. This involves a discussion of the way marketing is embedded in the society, how it functions as a source of social change, and how it is affected by social change. Marketing occurs in a variety of social contexts, whether these contexts are viewed in dichotomous terms such as public versus private, commercial versus noncommercial, profit versus nonprofit, and legal versus illegal, or in terms of multisectors such as education, population, social welfare, science, public policy, and law.

Chapter 4 delves more deeply into the nature of social conflict, discussing conflict as interpreted by various schools of thought. The issue has come to the fore especially of late, with arguments about whether the American society is based fundamentally on consensus or on conflict. Coser notes the shift from the image of society as an essentially peaceful adjustment between component parts to the assertion of the opposite extreme, that coercion and conflict are more basic social elements than consensus and equilibrium. He notes that order and disorder are intimately intertwined. The present volume agrees with this point of view, but explores the conflict element in particular in order to redress the balance, given the relative neglect of conflict as an issue in the marketing literature.

[10]Joseph A. Schumpeter, *The Theory of Economic Development* (Fair Lawn, N.J.: Oxford University Press, Galaxy, 1961), p. 9.

EXCHANGE AND CONFLICT

The idea of exchange has also not yet made much direct inroad into marketing literature. It tends to remain implicit or overlooked because the discussions are usually about the sellers' activities, with the aim of increasing their effectiveness; or about the consumers' behavior, again with the aim of increasing the sellers' effectiveness. A more objective analysis requires a balanced view, one that sees the constant mutuality of the exchange process at work. In this process, each participant has a complex of aims that are being translated into his marketing actions. These aims are satisfied in varying degrees but never totally. Each aim has a certain character in seeking satisfaction; it may require an object, a means, an expressiveness, an opportunity, a cost, or whatever. Conflict arises in the exchange process when there is some insufficiency or obstacle to the satisfaction—the marketplace does not seem to contain the precise object at the "right" price, there are barriers to the means sought, poor timing and missed opportunities, somehow a buyer or a seller, a group of buyers or sellers behaves in a way disapproved by others.

CONTEXTS OF CONFLICT

As a reaction to external circumstances, conflict is also a projection of various subjective states having to do with feelings of deprivation, specific and general frustrations, changing awarenesses and shifts in expectations. Internal conflict develops subjectively, with ambivalence about self-concepts and personal values. Over time values shift, satiation sets in, age-graded identifications arise, new informations and learnings are absorbed, with the end result of setting new aims at odds with old. This helps generate conflict. Conflicts arise because the aims of the sellers and the buyers are different and in some situations not necessarily complementary, resulting in some kind of thwarting. The rise of consumerism will be mentioned as a recent dramatic expression of the surfacing of certain kinds of conflicts. The differences of interest will be examined in various contexts, with instances that highlight the different assumptions, goals, and social values at work. Some particular instances are suggested:

1. The battle for the minds of children.
2. The ghetto consumer.
3. The case for and against advertising.
4. Selling morally controversial products.
5. Illegal marketing: the shadow system.

These and other examples will highlight how differences of interest occur among various social groups, including seller versus seller, seller versus buyer, and buyer versus buyer.

Chapter 6 concerns the management of marketing conflict. Conflict is a basic motor force, often leading individuals and formal and informal groups to get as much as they can while giving as little as possible. But "getting" and "giving" are defined very differently in different circumstances, and a maximum-minimum theory is too simple. Among diverse needs and motives are wishes to cooperate, to settle matters, to achieve mutually advantageous ends, etc. Without cooperation motivated by common interests among competing parties to resolve conflict nearly all social activity in which marketing is embedded would not take place, and social life would be very rudimentary at best. The intent of Chapter 6 is to analyze how marketing conflict, i.e., conflict in the giving and getting process, is resolved.

All the behavior of participants interacting in the marketing situation can be interpreted either as means of furthering a conflict or of ending it; but it is often not clear ahead of time which will be the result. The process is an ongoing one, with many battles, truces, and prisoners taken. But there is often no peace or final victory, and some victories Pyrrhic.

As there are many kinds of conflict, there are also many means of resolving them; the analysis can cut in various directions. The conflict may merely be stopped, or the differences may be dissolved. The results can be evaluated at the level of feeling, of verbalization, or of other nonverbal forms of action. The sources of resolution may be external (rules, third party) or arise in dyadic interaction.

Sidney J. Levy

Gerald Zaltman

Acknowledgments

We would particularly like to express our appreciation for the efforts of Richard Bagozzi, who was a constant source of input into various aspects of this book. He provided very valuable critiques, examples, alternative perspectives, and occasional proddings. Carol A. Scott, a doctoral student at the time this book was written, and Ruby Roy Dholakia also deserve mention for the assistance they provided at key points in this writing venture.

S.J.L. / G.Z.

CHAPTER ONE

The Growth
of Marketing

Marketing is a central human activity that has burgeoned dramatically in recent years. Paralleling its growth is the increasing intensity of stigmatism attached to the idea of marketing, and the disparagement of its methods and of the people who engage in it. This simultaneous attraction and repulsion defines a fascination and a warring of social impulses that require analysis and understanding, not merely taking sides. The present volume seeks to achieve these aims by exploring the role of conflict as a core variable in the marketing activities of society, examining its sources in the diverse social values held by different individuals and subgroups, as well as the means by which amelioration, consensus, and resolution come about.

The topic is of major importance to marketing, but one that has been given only piecemeal attention. The thesis of the present analysis is that marketing is a dynamic process in which various forms of conflict have for the most part been casually relegated to discussions of economic competition or noticed in particular situations when trouble flares up, whereas in fact conflict is an integral element and motor force in the marketing system.

Conflict in marketing goes on at all levels, from the intrapsychic to the international. Its presence is inherent, although it takes many forms and occurs in varying degrees. Because of its infinite variety, it has many names and will here be examined from numerous vantage points.

A brief backward look will help to locate the subject matter more precisely. Three aspects are interesting to distinguish: (1) the recent *evolution of marketing activity,* (2) the nature of society's *conceptualization and reactions to marketing,* and (3) the *growth of marketing study.*

The term *marketing* means many things, and there is little use in seeking to confine its meaning to a single definition; a broad one will be offered later, although in a sense the whole discussion aims to define marketing. It is necessary to struggle with the realization that the denotations and connotations of the word attest that marketing is an encompassing, protean idea. It refers to going shopping, to salesmanship, to the distribution of goods. To

1

some minds it means primarily advertising, or exploitation, venality, undue gain, and so forth. By examining the relationship of this concept to its place in society, perhaps increased light can be cast on its complexity.

EVOLUTION OF MARKETING ACTIVITY

The evolution of marketing activity is the evolution of the process of exchanges between and among people. Traditionally, these are referred to as economic exchanges, and economic conduct, according to Schumpeter, is "conduct directed toward the acquisition of goods."[1] But this is too narrow a description of marketing conduct, since it implies criteria for distinguishing this conduct from some other conduct that do not seem to withstand examination. For our purposes, each major word can be used, not to quarrel with Schumpeter, who had a great deal more to say on the subject, but as a departure point to show how unfettered an idea of marketing activities is required by their occurrence in modern life.

   Conduct must be understood to include not only physical actions that are motoric, overt, visible, as the word is ordinarily used. No behavior can be excluded from its participation in economic life whether or not expressed in outward actions. Ideas and emotions are inseparable from visible actions, as John Dewey thoroughly discussed long ago,[2] and play their prominent roles in marketers' concerns. The phrase *directed toward* need not be taken to imply too sharp a sense of purpose. Marketing activity includes stages of behavior that can seem so distant or vague in their relation to "marketing" that the impulse is to omit them. But even behaviors that seem aimless, withdrawn, undirected, merely self-expressive, and so forth, are forms of presentation or consumption that will require replenishment, and they go on in given environments with particular values. *Acquisition* implies information, availability, and access, one to acquire and therefore one to provide. *Marketing includes all that is done by those who want a customer and by those who want a seller.* Finally, what are *goods?* Common understanding interprets goods to mean products; the underlying reference is to anything one finds good. Such things need not, however, be generally viewed as virtuous, beneficial, or sound; the meaning of goods has to include "bads" also, such as pornographic films, cigarettes, and "Saturday night specials." Goods have also to be extended to include services as well as objects, where what is provided or gained are activities that occur in connection with products or are experiences, sensations, ideas, and emotions that people seek to have for their own sake.

   Even if the term *marketing* were limited to the traditional exchange of

---

[1]Joseph A. Schumpeter, *The Theory of Economic Development* (Fair Lawn, N.J.: Oxford University Press, 1961), p. 3.

[2]John Dewey, *Human Nature and Conduct* (New York: Modern Library, 1930).

products and money, its growth needs little demonstration. From the rude beginnings at crossroads to the vast contemporary marketing system, marketing activities have eleborated fantastically. The interested reader should consult Cyril Belshaw's *Traditional Exchange and Modern Markets* for a fascinating account of this.[3] They were always urged along by the roving spirit and its news of foreign marvels, stimulating the desire for exotic goods and the novel product. This is symbolized in the primal story of the purveying of the Original Apple and the awful price exacted for consuming it. In history, there is the voyaging of the Phoenician merchants and all the ancient ships setting out for spices, grain, cloth, art, and a growing volume of craft items. With the differential prevalence of resources and skills, gradients arose to establish trade routes across the known and into the unknown lands. The movement of goods took the customary forms of sharing, gift giving, looting, exacting tribute and taxes, and commercial trading.

In time, typical patterns arose—bazaars, marketplaces, famous centers of trade such as Crete in the period from 2500 B.C. to 1500 B.C. As the glory of Rome subsided and the feudal system engulfed Europe, the reliance on agriculture and self-subsistent domains reduced the vigor of marketing activity. But again, town growth gradually led to the market halls, to the trade fairs such as the famous Champagne Fair near Paris in the twelfth and thirteenth centuries. As the nation-states emerged and crystallized their mercantilist programs of exploration, colonization, and exploitation of natural resources, the national and international marketing system was richly developed. The convergences of historical events and forces that are called the Renaissance, the Enlightenment, and the Industrial Revolution provided the modern Western world with the cultural self-awareness, the social and economic philosophies, and the science and technology that continue to influence the contemporary era.[4] Recently added are the pressures due to intense population growth, atomic fission, and a changing cosmological view of the earth and its finite supply of materials and resources.

Marketing, both narrowly and broadly perceived, is essential to satisfying all the functional prerequisites of society. Marketing activities help people define tolerable *relationships with their environment* and is basic to *sexual recruitment.* Courtship is a marketing process basic to all societies including the "bride price" or "dowry"—and in highly modernized societies the "negotiated marriage contract," the most famous of which is the Kennedy-Onassis contract. Computer dating services are more marginal activities in this core area of social life. Another feature of a viable society is *role differentiation and role assignment.* Role differentiation and assignment is itself a market-

[3]Cyril S. Belshaw, *Traditional Exchange and Modern Markets* (Englewood Cliffs, N.J.: Prentice-Hall, Inc., 1965).

[4]For an exposition of the forces affecting economic development in modern times, applied to a specific local situation, see Clifford Geertz, *Peddlers and Princes* (Chicago: University of Chicago Press, 1963).

ing process but also one that marketers not directly involved in the context of the process are concerned with for promotional purposes. Marketers need to delineate such different roles as parent, child, decision maker, buyer, influencer, and so forth, and to understand the dynamics of such roles. *Communication* is another vital process that helps maintain a cohesive society. We need not dwell upon marketing as a communication process bringing together those who must sell and those who must buy. The mail-order form of merchandising is cited as a facilitating force in the development of rural America. Marketing activities also produce *shared ways of thinking* among members of a society. One interesting argument is that standardized products and services produce standardized thinking and behavior. This is suggested by persons who study the impact of technology upon society. A variant of this theme is that certain standardized needs determined through marketing research produce standardized products which reinforce and make more salient those particular needs and their associated thought processes. Several other functional prerequisites of society could be cited which can be viewed as marketing processes themselves as well as processes professional marketers need to understand and whose operation they facilitate. Some of these other prerequisites are shared articulated goals, normative regulation of means for achieving these goals, the regulation of effective expression, socialization, and the control of disruptive behavior.

CONCEPTUALIZATION AND REACTIONS TO MARKETING

By their very nature, the basic elements always present for marketing to occur have been parties to the exchange, locales, and a means of moving the values involved. What changes in marketing over time are such matters as *volume, form, emphasis,* and *meaning.* The volume of marketing activities has grown until current statistics are often casually cited in tons of goods and billions of dollars, and incalculable numbers of transactions. Testimony to this growth is easily gleaned from the daily press and trade media. Recent references were made to such miscellaneous illustrative facts as these: the temperature control industry (air conditioning, heating, and refrigeration) is a $12 billion industry; there is a $50 billion Delaware market, a $283 billion pension fund market. The bakery food industry boasts that it is the second largest segment of the food industry, with $10 billion in volume and with sales increasing twice as fast as population. Not to be outdone, the metal-working industry claims $10 billion a year for capital expenditures alone. In August 1973 the Conference Board summarized consumer market indicators for the United States to include 84.6 million employed persons with a total personal income of $1,019 billion.[5]

Such quantities require a far-flung marketing system, many intermedi-

[5]*Consumer Market Indicators* (The Conference Board, August 1973).

aries between producers and consumers, and constant transportation by vehicles capable of catering to extreme variations in weight, fragility, and temperature. Products and services keep finding novel forms as the inventiveness and the desires of the people keep changing the end goods in the marketplace or are changed further by the intervening products and services created to accommodate the process itself. The flow of information and persuasion in their own infinity of forms keeps enlarging to connect the ever-proliferating marketing locales which have grown from the concrete limitations of crossroads, single-town markets, and market halls to the endless exchange intersections formed by telephone lines and mail deliveries, to say nothing of all the plants, warehouses, stores, offices, homes, and vehicles where transactions occur.

In addition to the changes in forms of products, transportation methods, and communication media, there are shifts over time in emphasis on different aspects of marketing. To the local retail beginnings was added the role of wholesalers. The peddler carried the goods and the word, and then the traveling salesman fanned out to take wholesale orders. Such shifts show the changing locus of major marketing problems. Initially, in early, direct, face-to-face marketing contacts in local markets, transportation and communication were essential but needed less emphasis than the nature of the goods. When problems in any given sphere of production had been relatively mastered and delegated to specialists, marketing focus could shift to the wider dissemination and transportation of the goods. The progression of interest moved beyond narrow concern with basic commodities, exemplified in one of the government documents that appeared in 1901 around the time that formal study of marketing began: *Report of the Industrial Commission on the Distribution of Farm Products.* By 1922 one of the first marketing texts showed the emphasis on the transfer aspect with this definition of marketing: *Marketing consists of those efforts which effect transfers in the ownership of goods, and care for their physical distribution.*[6] Advertising began with whatever information was provided to prospective buyers, whether through shouting of wares or symbols of location, whether to announce mere availability or to appeal to the motives of members of the audience. In modern times, when the solutions to problems of production and transportation seem so sophisticated (despite the many unsolved ones), there has arisen an extravagant concern with the role of advertising as a focus of marketing. Coupled with it is intensive segmentation of the market, with vast sums being spent to cultivate markets of multitudinous stripes. For example, *Horseman,* the magazine of Western riding, recently solicited advertising by boasting of a paid subscriber list of 166,609 recreational horse owners all over North America. A direct-mail catalog offers the sale of lists of names of actual or potential market segments ranging from one live lion farm

[6]Fred E. Clark, *Principles of Marketing* (New York: The Macmillan Company, 1922), p. 1.

to 25,632,000 mail-order buyers in case one should wish to make marketing overtures to such as 21 bone black manufacturers, 503 book critics, 12 Albanian Orthodox churches, or 1,260 former Rhodes scholars, to say nothing of such ordinary segments as 250,000 attorneys, 19,000 bakers, or 10,000 office equipment dealers.

Reactions to marketing have altered along with changes of focus in the marketing system. As forms of social interaction, barter, trade, buying, and selling have always been intensely significant. The basic phenomenon of exchange tends to involve people's emotions strongly, inevitably including considerations of heightening or lowering satisfaction, self-esteem, and social status. One's economic condition is affected and ramifies into the individual and family life-style. The aim of gaining, of improving one's circumstances in the marketing of labor and in the expenditure of earnings, pervades social and economic philosophies and their expression in myths, folktales, and instruction in home and school.[7]

Although it is a thesis of the current work that all interactions may be interpreted from a marketing point of view, certain activities are traditionally demarcated as the role of the merchant, the seller, and special attitudes surround the idea of selling. Those who are specialized as sellers and the motives that are attributed to sellers have customarily been described in negative terms. A situation has a basic goodness about it when the traders are two producers exchanging goods for mutual convenience; and an ideal exchange is presumably one that benefits both parties equally. In such a trade of values, both persons are equally and simultaneously buyers and sellers in the sense of providing for a transfer of goods; but neither has to be perceived or stigmatized as a seller. When one has gained a greater value than the other, he can be regarded as being smarter, shrewder, more alert, and so forth, but he also exposes himself to charges of being greedy, exploitative, and inclined to take advantage. Where the middleman arises and money is involved, motives become especially sensitive. Some financial profit may be regarded as fair, in recognition of the costs of certain inputs and distribution services. But the distributor becomes divorced from basic production and is associated more narrowly with the goals of gaining and accumulating as much money as possible. This motive is taken as unusually egocentric and damaging to other people, and therefore deserving of less admiration than other vocational aims—to grow or create goods, to study, to fight, to be aesthetically self-expressive, to heal, and even to attempt to govern. Historically, degradation and distortion of personal and social values have been implied by more concern with money than with real goods and constructive

---

[7]The complex of motives and their relative importance in different countries is well illustrated in the work of David C. McClelland, *The Achieving Society* (New York: Van Nostrand Reinhold Co., 1961).

goals, reaching their nadir in those who trade in money itself, who lend and charge interest.[8]

The intervention of money has a curious effect on the interpretation of human motives. To ask for money in return for one's product or service introduces an impersonal, unloving element. It is interpreted to mean that providing the good is not done with intrinsic enjoyment, generosity, or desire to please or even to receive gratitude. The *amateur,* by definition, provides commodities for the love of it, but to ask for money is a sign of coldness. The money (or the other things that the money will buy) is what is loved, not the activity, the product, or the recipient. It is interesting to note, however, that even among the very poor in some countries there is a preference for paying a small sum of money for contraceptives, for example, as opposed to receiving them free. This may be because quality is inferred from price or because personal dignity is maintained or for other reasons. Thus in some instances people want to give cash despite the generosity of donor agencies. This raises the interesting situation where the donor agency is being indifferent, despite its noble intentions, to the needs or wants of some of the people it serves. The deflection of interest implied is the snake in the Eden of exchanges, leading to ideas of selling as base and carrying the evil connotations of prostitution and meretriciousness, of being mercenary, of "selling out" as betrayal, of commercial art as inferior to fine art (even though the work itself might be the same).

In any given society there are mixed attitudes about these negative ideas. Ceilings on interest still linger, but credit, interest, and dividends are given almost full sway; one is uncertain whether to marvel at any given percentages. As W. Lloyd Warner points out, the different sources of income are valued differently. Commonly, inherited wealth is envied and elevates one's social status compared to profits and fees, with these in turn superior to salary and wages.[9] The nature of one's clientele is important in judging the marketer. The artist with a princely patron could be more esteemed than the artist in a modern advertising agency.[10] Commercial behavior develops differentiations: for example, haggling skill is enjoyed and admired in the Middle East, and the status of the entrepreneur varies considerably with the culture of various countries. Richard N. Farmer in his provocative article, "Would You Want Your Daughter to Marry a Marketing Man?,"[11] sug-

---

[8] See John Ruskin, "Usury," *Contemporary Review,* Vol. 37 (February 1880), for diatribe against notion of money breeding money. Equally vainly, perhaps, he sought to find the merchant's *raison d'être* not in profit, but in *providing.* See "Unto This Last," *Cornhill Magazine* (1862).

[9] W. Lloyd Warner *et al., Social Class in America* (Chicago: Science Research Associates, 1949).

[10] Although the latter might well feel more self-respect when reading Mozart's pathetic letters preoccupied with his money problems and begging.

[11] *Journal of Marketing,* 31 (January 1967), 1-3.

gests that marketing, as many people see it anyway, is both unethical and irrelevant. He sums up very nicely an attitude prevailing widely in society: "If that nice young man who has dates with your daughter turns out to be a marketing major, what would you do? I would chase him off the premises fast. Who wants his daughter to marry a marketer?" [12]

Rostow points to the role of science, innovations, material advance, and other propensities in economic development.[13] Arthur Cole suggests four main elements whose variations among social systems have marked impact on entrepreneurial performance and how it is received or evaluated in the community. These elements are acceptance of change, opportunities for social mobility, tolerance of money making, and attitudes toward material accumulation or conspicuous consumption.[14] He compares the United States, France, and England for their varied emphases, with France highlighting the relationship of wealth to the family, its honor and reputation, resulting in a kind of continuation of the feudal, manorial estate, diminishing personal advantage and competitiveness. In England, mercantile domination of the towns was more pronounced, coupled with the entrepreneurs' ambitions to be admitted to the high society of the landed gentry and Parliament, keeping rivalry within mannered bounds and mere wealth at a disadvantage.

In the United States, the recency of an aristocracy, and the openness of the frontier and its secular character, fostered the rise of new kinds of heroes, among whom was the man who could make money.

> The unique force of money income as a motivation in our society appears to arise from the fact that the social recognition and the self-respect achieved by an individual are largely dependent on the degree of occupational success which he achieves. . . .[15]

That is, in the United States the great acceptance of change, with social mobility as a byword, tended to diminish the Old World restraints of established status and the traditional deference given to the clergy, soldiers, rulers, teachers, and professionals. "From rags to riches" became an honorific idea, one to which a man could apply single-minded devotion in seeking to supply a growing nation with mass-produced goods and especially making possible the country's tremendous distributive achievement.[16]

The American salesman became a symbol that represented the marketing

[12]*Ibid.*, p. 3.

[13]Walt W. Rostow, *The Process of Economic Growth* (New York: W. W. Norton & Company, Inc., 1952).

[14]Arthur H. Cole, *Business Enterprise in Its Social Setting* (Cambridge: Harvard University Press, 1959), pp. 148-49.

[15]James S. Duesenberry, "Some Aspects of the Theory of Economic Development," in *Explorations in Entrepreneurial History,* 3, No. 73 (1950-51), p. 72.

[16]Walter Hoving, *The Distribution Revolution* (New York: Ives Washburn, Inc., 1960).

skills and orientation, the energy and drive, the sociability and persuasiveness that came to typify the nation. While not universally admired, the salesman was widely welcomed. Steady growth in the standard of living as the wealth of the country grew was fueled by the desire to consume and accumulate goods and services. Advertising played a major role in making known what was available and in stimulating the desire for particular goods. Initially, it received no great general blame for doing so. It seemed taken for granted that people had needs and wants that could include more than stark food and shelter. Rich elites have almost always been motivated toward elaborating their diets in quantity and variety, dressing opulently, building and furnishing large and comfortable dwellings, collecting art and hobbies, and indulging their leisure. Advertising was not required to spur the avarice of Jack climbing the beanstalk or of Cinderella dreaming of a glittering party dress. It *was* needed to show what fashions of dress were available and how gold might be spent, to instruct the less imaginative about the possibilities of diversifying consumption. As David Potter has suggested, by equating the opportunity for abundance with democracy and freedom, material advance was ennobled, and with it the marketing system.[17]

Of course, the relative degradation of materialism remained, compared to more intangible and less "animal" strivings, and almost at the same time as the relative exaltation of the salesman was occurring, the seeds of decline in his reputation appeared. The American salesman was so urgently motivated toward success that he was quickly perceived as going to extremes. The men who could sell anything included those who tried—patent medicines, gold bricks, the Brooklyn Bridge. American hyperbole joined with unscrupulousness and guilefulness to overlap the salesman with the confidence man. Similarly with advertising, its initial quiet, informative approach soon included exaggerated consumer benefits. Russell Lynes notes that there were no professional copywriters in 1840:

> Each merchant wrote his own advertisements, which were, except for the scandalous claims of hundreds of patent medicines and contraceptive powders and pills, merely lists of items for sale with their prices.[18]

Scandals in the conduct of business have never been novel. As men set out to gain success and wealth, whether it be the ancient philosopher Thales cornering a market or the nineteenth-century robber barons, the attitude of "public be damned" finds expression in swindles, indifference to product quality, terrible service, discriminatory practices, price fixing, and land steals. Indignation and exposures by Upton Sinclair, Ida Tarbell, and others highlighted the evils in various industries. Such evils are not always self-

---

[17]David M. Potter, *People of Plenty: Economic Abundance and the American Character* (Chicago: University of Chicago Press, 1954).

[18]Russell Lynes, *The Tastemakers* (New York: Harper & Bros., 1954), p. 11.

evident or familiar to the public. The writers, viewing with alarm, pointed them out and supplied the rhetoric, the emotion, and the public shame that fueled others into action. Changes occurred in the definition of what are *fair* prices, *pure* ingredients, *unfair* competition, and the degree of government intervention required to control and police them. Regulatory agencies burgeoned, spurred by the growth of federal power during the Franklin D. Roosevelt years, met by the swelling of corporations with professional managers rather than the traditional aggressive entrepreneurs.

With the post-World War II surge of productivity and the consequent affluent buyers' market, there was a general sense of a process coming to fruition. Life in the United States seemed bountiful and merchants seemed oriented to the role of *providing,* almost as Ruskin envisioned it. Products were increasingly designed to make things easy, comfortable, colorful, and varied. The vision of the Good Life for all, with almost universal education and the proliferation of single-family dwellings in suburban idylls, came to dominate the fantasies and aspirations of the mass market.

In the 1950s fresh difficulties became evident. One harbinger was the popular identification with David Riesman's *The Lonely Crowd.*[19] Its lament at the emergence of other-directedness as the predominant American personality trait met with widespread agreement, even by those who echoed sadly to the title and did not read the book. But other-directedness can also be taken as an essential feature of rapid economic development, as McClelland indicates, making for orderly social behavior, flexibility in adaptations to change, and a market morality that is responsive to public opinion.[20]

More generally, other-directedness is interpreted as a loss of stable traditions and autonomy, as an impersonal and alienated dependency on passing currents. The individual's vulnerability to "others" thus became the occasion for alarm, expressed and spurred by Vance Packard's widespread success, *The Hidden Persuaders,* a book purporting to expose the presence of insidious forces seeking to manipulate the consumers' desires. Another sign of the marketing system's being viewed as generally inimical to the interests of the community was Galbraith's *The Affluent Society.*[21] Designed to reveal some of the ills of the day (like R. H. Tawney's *The Acquisitive Society,* originally titled *Sickness of the Acquisitive Society*), he there began to develop the idea that advertising had a squirrel wheel effect in making the people want the things the corporations wanted to produce, at the expense of public sector benefits. He terms this process the *dependence effect.*[22] As these and other

[19]David Riesman *et al., The Lonely Crowd* (New Haven, Conn.: Yale University Press, 1950).

[20]David C. McClelland, *The Achieving Society* (New York: Van Nostrand, 1961), pp. 192-97.

[21]John K. Galbraith, *The Affluent Society* (Boston: Houghton Mifflin Company, 1958).

[22]*Ibid.,* p. 158.

critics became increasingly vocal, the public gained instruction and rein-forcement in negative attitudes toward marketing. The proportions express-ing discontent with products, prices, services, and advertising rose in public opinion surveys, culminating in the movement called *consumerism* under the leadership of Ralph Nader.

The focal changes in marketing and the concomitant shifts in public attitudes reflect an ambivalent and a paradoxical situation. The ambivalence comes about because the public does feel a sense of success and progress stimulated by the flow of goods and the seeming chance to amplify one's total sum of satisfaction but is simultaneously faced with endless incentives toward further production, acquisition, and consumption. The consumers are para-doxically increasingly discontent and critical, willing to support Nader, class action suits, and the growing multitude of critics all the more as the market-ing system has changed toward creating mass distribution and its economies of scale, researching the needs of consumers, providing more choices for more varied market segments, and intensifying communications of appeals and availability of goods.

GROWTH OF MARKETING STUDY

The growth of marketing study has paralleled certain of the above develop-ments. Robert Bartels established a developmental conceptualization in his book *The Development of Marketing Thought.*[23] He shows how the word *marketing* was first used as a noun around 1900 and terms the first decade of the century the *Period of Discovery.* This and successive periods are summed up as follows:

1900-1910—*Period of Discovery.* Initial teachers of marketing sought facts about the distributive trades. Theory was borrowed from economics relating to distribution, world trade, and commodity markets. The conception of "mar-keting" occurred, and a name was given to it.

• • •

1910-20—*Period of Conceptualization.* Many marketing concepts were initially developed. Concepts were classified, and terms were defined.

• • •

1920-30—*Period of Integration.* Principles of marketing were postulated, and the general body of thought was integrated for the first time.

• • •

1930-40—*Period of Development.* Specialized areas of marketing continued to be developed, hypothetical assumptions were verified and quantified, and some new approaches to the explanation of marketing were undertaken.

• • •

[23]Robert Bartels, *The Development of Marketing Thought* (Homewood, Ill.: Richard D. Irwin, Inc., 1962).

1940-50—*Period of Reappraisal.* The concept and traditional explanation of marketing was reappraised in terms of new needs for marketing knowledge. The scientific aspects of the subject were considered.

•   •   •

1950-60—*Period of Reconception.* Traditional approaches to the study of marketing were supplemented by increasing emphasis upon managerial decision making, the societal aspects of marketing, and quantitative marketing analysis. Many new concepts, some borrowed from the field of management and from other social sciences, were introduced into marketing.[24]

Marketing study grew through the accretion of ideas from many sources and pressed outward to encompass ever additional spheres of inquiry. One result has been the increasing divergence in the meaning of marketing to the various participants in the marketing system. The critical public and professional critics tend to equate marketing with the idea of "hard sell," especially accomplished by means of misleading and overly persuasive advertising. Business practitioners of marketing think of marketing mainly as whatever they do to bring their products and services to their customers and to consummate transactions with them. The consumer thinks of *going* marketing rather than *doing* it, thus referring to shopping and buying.

All such perspectives received reinforcement after World War II. The shift in relative emphasis from production orientation to consumer orientation that came about then was a milestone in marketing history. This shift, termed *the marketing concept,* provided a rationale for a new emphasis on marketing activities, as distinguished from merely "selling." Supposedly signaling a turn away from aggressive determination to "force" customers to buy goods because they had been produced and needed to be sold, the marketing literature exhorted marketers to do marketing research, to "satisfy needs," to "think customer," and so forth. This literature produced a struggle between reality and philosophy, as many companies gave lip service to these new ideas in marketing but persisted in their usual practices.

EXCURSUS ON SELLING AND THE MARKETING CONCEPT

What is the marketing concept? Roughly stated, the marketing concept called for a customer orientation on the part of the firm, backed by an integrated marketing effort designed to assure customer satisfaction as a means of obtaining long-term profit. The marketing process was to begin and end with the consumer. As a business philosophy, the marketing concept was seen as a distinct departure from the traditional sales orientation in which it was the seller's job to get the buyer to accept the seller's point of view. [25] Recently, however, questions about the marketing process have been raised

[24]*Ibid.,* p. 41.

[25]Robert Bartels, *Marketing Theory and Metatheory* (Homewood, Ill.: Richard D. Irwin, Inc., 1970).

which suggest that perhaps the marketing concept has failed to affect significantly the relationship between consumer and marketer.

The roots of the *sales orientation* lie in the early conceptualizations of marketing as being synonymous with distribution, and as serving the function of finding outlets for society's productive resources. Marketing was completely divorced from production decisions; without a sale, no marketing had occurred.[26] Whatever could be produced had to be sold as efficiently as possible. The most obvious variables under the marketer's control to accomplish this objective were advertising and the sales force, both of which received considerable attention in the literature and textbooks.

The notion of a sales orientation is associated with short-term company objectives. It did not explicitly recognize the implications of sales efforts for repeat purchases, the building of consumer franchises, or the ultimate satisfaction of the consumer. The marketer's responsibility began and ended with the sales transaction. The criteria for evaluating a marketer's performance were the sales data.

The marketing concept sought to alter this orientation in several ways. First, the marketing effort would be integrated with production decisions. Now the job of the marketer included anticipating consumer needs and wants, determining the volume of the anticipated demand, and relaying this information to the production division so that the firm could produce what the consumer desired. Second, the marketing concept explicitly recognized the economic value of satisfying the customer. This meant that the firm had to look beyond the point of purchase; it had to produce the kind of product that a consumer would want to buy again. Third, the volume of *profit*, not solely sales, would be the new criterion for evaluation. This meant a further integration of the firm's management to ensure that the firm's resources would produce profitable items, not merely those that would sell. Profitability was to be the operational measure of consumer satisfaction.

Can one then say that the essence of marketing, under the marketing concept, is not the sales transaction? From one viewpoint, the answer is no. One could argue that the marketing concept was designed to facilitate sales. The selling function could be performed more easily and more efficiently if the firm were producing goods and services that the consumer already wanted. As a marketing management technique, anticipating and satisfying consumer wants and needs proved to be highly effective. It could be justified in economic terms by stating that demand influenced supply, scarce resources were allocated in a manner consistent with demand, and thus the welfare of society would be increased. From another perspective, the marketing concept was interpreted to mean that the importance of the sales function would be overridden by consumer considerations. Adopting the marketing concept, at

---

[26]Roland S. Vaile, E. T. Grether, and Reavis Cox, *Marketing in the American Economy* (New York: The Ronald Press Company, 1952).

least from the consumer's point of view, meant that business recognized and submitted to ultimate control by society.

By more closely examining these two conflicting points of view, one can see why there is growing disenchantment with adopting the view of marketing as reflected in the marketing concept alone. Firms successfully implementing the marketing concept did prosper, and for the most part, consumers benefited as well. New products proliferated, distribution made shopping more convenient, and packages were designed for protection of the product and ease in use and disposal (at least for the consumer himself). In short, the needs and wants that the individual himself could articulate were more closely matched with the product offerings. In the sixties, however, the phenomenon of consumer unrest and dissatisfaction known as consumerism began to grow. Factors contributing to the rise of consumerism in the sixties are shown in Table 1-1. Consumers became extremely vocal about how well their interests were being served. For the firm that had been spending thousands of dollars on consumer research in order to better serve them, consumerism was a bit of a surprise. There was some discussion about who had really implemented the marketing concept. Peter Drucker called consumerism "the shame of the total marketing concept," with the implication that the concept had been implemented in name only.[27] More recently, students of marketing have begun to study the possibility that the marketing concept has inherent limitations in its ability to solve societal problems.

The first difficulty with the marketing concept lies in a basic misunderstanding. Consumer research was not designed merely to guarantee sales, nor were consumer interests to take precedence over the profitability of the firm. Rather, the marketing concept stated the interdependence of these two factors. Profits would not be generated if consumers were not offered something of value, and conversely, consumers would not be provided with goods and services unless the firm received profits. The marketing concept, as a *marketing management* philosophy, did not specify that either party to the marketing process served solely for the other. Both parties were to exist in a *mutually* beneficial relationship. Bell and Emory have suggested that the problem was simply a reversal of goals: marketers should seek to identify consumer needs first, rather than profits.[28] Unfortunately, this does not resolve the basic exchange nature of marketing, since ultimately those needs that cannot be profitably filled will be ignored by private marketing managers.

Related to this is the fact that marketing, as reflected in the marketing concept, deals essentially with *individuals* and clusters of customers, and not with the aggregate of individuals termed *society*. The marketing concept is a

[27]Peter F. Drucker, "The Shame of Marketing," *Marketing/Communications,* August 1969, p. 60.

[28]Martin L. Bell and C. William Emory, "The Faltering Marketing Concept," *Journal of Marketing,* 35 (October 1971), 37-42.

TABLE 1-1

Factors Contributing to the Rise of Consumerism in the Sixties

(1) *Structural Conduciveness*	(2) *Structural Strain*	(3) *Growth of a Generalized Belief*	(4) *Precipitating Factors*	(5) *Mobilization for Action*	(6) *Social Control*
Advancing incomes and education	Economic discontent (inflation)	Social critic writings (Galbraith, Packard, Carson, and so on.)	Professional agitation (Nader, and so on.)	Mass media coverage	Business resistance or indifference
Advancing complexity of technology and marketing	Social discontent (war and race)	Consumer-oriented legislators (Kefauver, Douglas, and so on.)	Spontaneous agitation (housewife picketing, and so on.)	Vote-seeking politicians	Legislative resistance or indifference
Advancing exploitation of the environment	Ecological discontent (pollution)	Presidential messages		New consumer interest groups and organizations	
	Marketing system discontent (shoddy products, gimmickry, dishonesty)	Consumer organizations			
	Political discontent (unresponsive politicians and institutions)				

Source: Philip Kotler, "What Consumerism Means to Marketers," *Harvard Business Review*, May-June 1972, p. 51.

philosophy to be adopted by individual firms and has implications for the practice of marketing management as it seeks to deal with its consumers on an individual basis. From a marketing management point of view, the marketing concept states the responsibility of the firm to satisfy consumers. On the surface, it may seem as if consumers are society, and, of course, society is the sum of consumers. However, society is not a simple sum of its parts. What seems desirable from the point of view of individual producers or consumers acting in their own best interests may be undesirable for the society as a whole.[29] Fulfillment of society's needs, such as for a cleaner landscape, may be directly contradictory to the individual's desires, such as convenience in disposing of containers.[30] Under the marketing concept as originally formulated, the marketing manager is not held responsible for satisfying the needs of society.

To correct part of this gap in understanding, Kotler has proposed a societal concept of marketing.[31] The societal concept of marketing "calls for a *customer orientation* backed by *integrated* marketing aimed at generating customer satisfaction and long-run consumer welfare as the key to attaining the long-run profitable volume." Kotler suggests that this concept be implemented by offering for sale products that have both attractive and pleasing short-term qualities, as well as salutary long-term benefits. Adding nutritional ingredients to already tasty and attractive snack foods would create this type of product. Providing a low-phosphate detergent with cleaning power equal to that of phosphate detergents is another example. By designing products with these attributes, marketing managers can serve the interests of consumers and society.

Societal implications notwithstanding, this new concept of marketing does not remove the essential nature of marketing as an exchange process whose core is a sale. Kotler calls upon marketers to be more innovative in their product research, to add more value to their offerings. He does not argue that profits be considered inconsequential or that sales figures be ignored. Stimulation of sales may even become more important, since societal welfare may depend upon consumer acceptance of such products, and because of their higher cost, these products may meet with more resistance. The profit motive is still the mechanism by which marketers are induced to provide these products. Where profitability cannot be achieved, the marketing mechanism is presumably inoperative. Again, one could say that marketing management is a technique or a set of techniques designed to facilitate sales. Are we still operating under a sales orientation? Are there actually any real differences between selling and marketing?

[29]Y. Hugh Furuhashi and E. Jerome McCarthy, *Social Issues of Marketing in the American Economy* (Columbus, Ohio: Grid, Inc., 1971).

[30]Robert P. Hammond, "Oregon Retailers Pop Tops over Beverage Refund Laws," *Supermarketing,* February 1973, pp. 1, 14-15.

[31]Philip Kotler, "What Consumerism Means for Marketers," *Harvard Business Review,* May-June 1972.

To say that the difference between marketing and selling lies in the sales transaction is misleading. Marketing includes, as a very important component, the sales transaction. The differences between the two perspectives, however, are several. First, marketing recognizes the inherent interdependencies of consumers and marketing managers. A selling orientation views business and consumers as two separate, and opposing, forces; business supposedly can exist as a separate entity as long as it can persuade consumers to buy what it makes or limit the range of choice. Second, and perhaps most important, marketing recognizes that the firm must deal with consumers in several situations. For a selling orientation, only one interface with the consumer is necessary, the point of purchase. A marketing perspective indicates that marketers and consumers must communicate on many levels and at various times throughout the marketing process. Besides communicating *to* the consumer through advertising and at the time of purchase, marketers must communicate *with* the consumer during the research or planning phase. Consumer thoughts must actively be sought by the marketer. Thus marketing recognizes communication as a two-way street. Marketing research has grown tremendously in the past two decades in trying to fill this need. Third, marketing views, as part of its responsibility, pulling the firm in line with consumer viewpoints. Through the communication process, it is hoped that this realignment is an anticipatory action rather than a defensive reaction. Thus the allocation of scarce resources will proceed in the direction of consumer dictates in a more efficient manner.

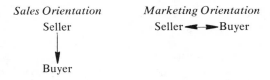

Unfortunately, this does not solve the problem completely. Questions remain to be answered, even if we restrict our discussion to marketing as a management technique and set aside for a while the social system dimension of marketing. Under a marketing orientation, the consumer is given a voice in the decision-making process. But how articulate is this voice? Is it the responsibility of the marketing research arm to discover needs that the consumer cannot articulate? Can he voice the need for a "safe" cigarette if he does not know that the one he smokes is dangerous to his health? Can we rely on the consumer always to know what is in his best interest? How much responsibility should be placed on the marketer to discover these latent needs?

Suppose a need could be identified whose fulfillment would be in the interests of consumer and societal welfare. Is it the responsibility of the marketing manager to override the marketplace vote of the consumer, the right to elect not to purchase, through an aggressive sales approach? Gelb and Brien, in their discussion of marketing at *Survival U.*, suggest that it will be the marketing practitioner's job to ensure survival regardless of the consumer vote.[32] Will the range of alternatives offered the consumer exclude the option of not buying? The argument of the end justifying the means seems to be very much alive.

Finally, is the marketing research approach to communication adequate? The housewife, for example, has been researched almost to the point of irritation. Researchers are finding it increasingly difficult to obtain interviews. This is caused in part by the not uncommon practice of conducting false interviews as part of a selling process. Data exist that "false market surveys have a deleterious effect upon respondent willingness to cooperate in subsequent market research studies."[33] Yet housewives continue to be quite vocal in their criticism of the marketplace. Increasingly, consumers feel powerless to communicate their frustrations and anxieties. Perhaps research has been carried out, not from the perspective of trying to know the consumer, but from the view of knowing the consumer's answers to management's questions. Marketing researchers must be careful not to rule out areas of discontent by the form of their questionnaires. Do marketing researchers need a "We Listen Better" campaign to jog them out of stereotypic ruts? Clearly, from the marketing concept perspective, it is incumbent upon the researcher to ask the right questions and to develop the art of listening.

The marketing concept and the societal marketing concept imply that the consumer should be on an equal footing with the marketer. The question is whether that amorphous group known as consumers possesses sufficient countervailing power. From a marketing management view, as long as the marketer keeps the lines of communication open, he has done his job. Third-party groups must take on the responsibility of seeing that all possible alternatives are considered and the consumers do possess a countervailing and controlling power. The marketer must talk with the consumer, but someone else must educate him. Then again, one marketer has argued that consumers are themselves quite Machiavellian.

On the behavioral side, marketing study shows new emphasis in these directions:

- How to *position* products and brands to maximize their distinctive interest to buyers
- Continued *analyses of consumers* under the headings of "psychographics" and "life-style"
- Intensified study of how to change and measure attitudes

[32]Betsy D. Gelb and Richard H. Brien, "Survival and Social Responsibility: Themes for Marketing Education and Management," *Journal of Marketing,* 35, No. 2 (April 1971), 3-9.

[33]Thomas Sheets *et al.,* "Deceived Respondents: Once Bitten, Twice Shy," *Public Opinion Quarterly,* 38 (Summer 1974), 261-63.

- Broadening of the concept of marketing to encompass its application to all other organizations, and "social marketing" of products, services, and ideas in the not-for-profit realms
- Debate over the need for business to consider its *social responsibilities* to its product development and its appeals to customers

Most contemporary approaches to marketing study, however, use a relatively static or nondynamic conceptualization of people. Many workers seek to replace or to go beyond the traditional model of economic man, narrowly motivated by price, but are uncertain about what to use in its stead. The newer models are enriched by inclusion of a greater number of variables— though often being little more than compendiums of labeled rectangular boxes. The people are conceived of as essentially wooden bundles of traits or attitudes, with simple emotions of anxiety and satisfaction. Some supposed sophistication or complexity comes from going beyond correlating two variables, using techniques of multidimensional analysis, clustering and factoring, with modest results to date. Others avoid the problems of analyzing motives by restricting their interest to external behavior, studying markets only as aggregates of demographic characteristics or as impersonal entities with probabilistic chances of acting. When motives are introduced, they are likely to be treated as unidimensional scales, sometimes as having the attributes of vectors, but rarely with due respect for their real life manifestations. Formal academic research in marketing has the freedom to explore systematic relationships out of context, so to speak, since it is not trying to cope with the total situation as the marketing manager has to do. As a consequence, the less rigorous practical marketing research, which is aimed at assisting immediate decision making, commonly explores more richly the way social and psychological forces are operating in the marketplace. Such exploration draws heavily on the traditions of social science inquiry, especially as found in survey methods, in field observations and intensive interviewing, and in analysis of projective materials. The further discussion presented here partakes of this orientation, being grounded in informal observation of the business and social scenes, and analysis of forces at work in some significant marketing areas.

Table 1-2 is a summary of representative perspectives of marketing emerging during the late 1960s and early 1970s. The reader will note the heavy emphasis on marketing as a social phenomenon having impact on other social phenomena. The general thrust of most writing in the last few years has been to break out of the traditional domains of marketing—without neglecting them—and to be sensitive to (1) opportunities to study and apply marketing in nontraditional settings and (2) the effect of traditional marketing on the broader aspects of life in society.

TABLE 1-2

Summary of Representative Papers on Marketing as a Discipline

Author	Theme	Basic Idea(s)
Bartels (1965)	Marketing is a social process.	Marketing is a social process "whereby society is fulfilling the personal and institutional needs of the society for physical or consumption goods and services." This view emphasizes the importance of the cultural roles, relationships, and values of business organizations. In such a context marketing thought becomes one of several guides to action. In an advanced society like the U.S. where there are many business roles and relationships, the task of marketing management is to coordinate and balance these various roles and relationships.
Bartels (1968)	A general theory of marketing is possible, given an appropriate definition of marketing.	A need is expressed for a general theory of marketing which will be able to integrate existing and forthcoming knowledge at higher levels of unification and abstraction. Marketing is defined as the process "whereby society, to supply its consumption needs, evolves distributive systems composed of participants, who, interacting under constraints—technical (economic) and ethical (social)—creates transactions or flows which resolve market separations and result in exchange and consumption." This definition of marketing is believed by the author to provide a foundation for a general theory of marketing.
Kotler and Levy (1969)	Marketing is applicable to, and performed by, nonbusiness organizations.	Although marketing is traditionally associated with activities of business firms, it is a more pervasive societal activity performed by different organizations in a wide variety of contexts. Political parties, museums, churches, universities all have products, markets, and marketing tools, but it is the business organization that has developed and used the science of effective marketing management. Marketing principles based on such concepts as generic product definition, target groups definition, differentiated marketing, customer behavior analysis, differential advantages, integrated marketing planning, and marketing audit can be adapted and used equally effectively by nonbusiness organizations.

Lewis and Erickson
(1969)

Functional and systems approaches

Functional and systems approaches are two of several approaches used in the study of marketing. Lewis and Erickson redefine the functional approach by identifying marketing functions with unique and inherent purposes of the marketing process. Two such functions are identified—to obtain and to service demand. To accomplish the two fundamental purposes, marketing activities are listed which accomplish one or both of them.

While the systems approach has gained in popularity and is advanced as an alternative approach to the study of marketing, the two approaches are intimately related. The purposes (functions) and activities of marketing identified in the functional approach define the input and output objects in the systems approach which then builds on it in terms of other objects (processes, feedback, control), their attributes and relationships. Thus the functional approach becomes a prerequisite to the systems approach, and the two together provide a consistent framework for classifying, designing, and analyzing marketing activities.

Robin
(1970)

Need for normative marketing

Positive science has been emphasized to develop marketing as a scientific discipline. Positive science involves the explanation, prediction, and control of phenomena without an ethical or normative position. This creates a problem, since the phenomenon of most interest to marketers is consumer behavior, and development of a positive science in marketing means an increasing infringement of human privacy.

In the absence of a normative science, a situation may develop where infringement of privacy exceeds the benefits of increased efficiency derived from better explanation, prediction, and control. Legislation may be enacted to prevent further infringement, but not when it is most optimal. To achieve the goal of total consumer satisfaction requires development of a normative science in marketing which will consist of application of scientific principles according to ethical and moral goals, i.e., "what ought to be."

Table 1-2 *(cont.)*

Author	Theme	Basic Idea(s)
Kotler and Zaltman (1971)	Marketing is a tool for planned social change.	The view of marketing as an action technology expands the domain in which it can be applied. It is natural that the logic of marketing will be applied to social goals, but certain conditions are necessary for successful social marketing. Social marketing requires careful planning and is defined as "the design, implementation and control of programs calculated to influence the acceptability of social ideas and involving considerations of product planning, pricing, communication, distribution and marketing research." The core idea is the same as in business planning: managing the exchange process.
Feldman (1971)	Marketing must adapt to changing societal needs.	Marketing systems have been very successful in delivering goods and services in quantity, quality, and variety. But the societal implications of these activities have not always been favorable. Marketing needs to respond to these conditions by emphasizing nonmaterial consumption, stressing societal criteria for purchase and consumption, and participating in centralized planning of policies that affect marketing. These changes would be necessary as the government (and not the market) becomes stronger in making decisions and groups use power in fulfilling their rights.
Dawson (1971)	Marketing has wrongfully neglected significant social issues.	The lack of well-defined boundaries of marketing and the neglect of significant social issues have created problems for the field. While increasingly viewed as a social process, marketing has failed to develop along lines that would promote society's goals. These problems have been created by three factors: (1) promoting marketing as a science that emphasizes methodology (experimentation, quantification), (2) undertaking "practical" research with visible payoffs, and (3) viewing the world in terms of markets and consumers, which neglects the *human.*
Kotler 1972	Marketing should be viewed as a transactional process.	The generic concept of marketing is concerned with "how transactions are created, stimulated, facilitated, and valued." The focus is on *transaction,* which is "the exchange of values between two

22

parties." Thus marketing takes place whenever (1) there are two social units, (2) one is seeking a specific response from another, (3) the response probability is not fixed, and (4) one attempts to produce the desired response by creating and offering values to the market. By adopting a functional view of marketing, the generic concept does not limit marketing to specific institutions (such as business organizations), to specific responses (such as purchase behavior), or to specific response units (such as consumers).

Sweeney (1972)

Marketing is a societal process as well as a technology.

The exchange process is accepted as the fundamental idea in marketing, but a conflict is created between the view of marketing as a social process (with focus on exchange process) and the view of marketing as a technology employed to execute exchange processes. The concept of marketing is a function of its proponents' perspective, and three levels of social aggregation (or perspective) determine the definition of marketing: the organizational system, the distribution system, and the social system. The social system perspective is superior because it views marketing not only as a technology or economic process but also as a "fundamental societal process which necessarily and inherently evolves within a society to facilitate the effectiveness and efficient resolution of the society's needs for exchange of consumption values."

This perspective relates technology, organization, and systems at a higher level or aggregation, views marketing as an interactive process, and indicates societal values as the criteria for evaluating marketing effectiveness.

Stidsen and Schulte (1972)

Marketing is basically a communication process.

The marketing concept as it has been operationalized does not reflect its true spirit. It emphasizes specific outcomes rather than the process; it represents itself as a well-implemented monologue rather than facilitating a dialogue. If the marketing concept is operationalized as a communication process, it will overcome these limitations because "the ideal marketing process is a functioning dialogue involving a communication system which enables consumers and producers to significantly influence each other's goal attainment."

23

Table 1-2 (cont.)

Author	Theme	Basic Idea(s)
Enis (1973)	Marketing theory requires more empirical tests.	Several concepts in marketing have been abstractly stated but inadequately operationalized. Theory building requires both conceptualization and empirical investigation of hypotheses. To bridge the gap between theory building and theory testing requires deepening the concept of marketing which "entails developing operational marketing theories and testing them in real marketing situations."
Kernan (1973)	Requirements for a mature discipline	Marketing will be a mature discipline when it possesses three characteristics—the study of the discipline is scientifically based, the practice of the discipline is unrestricted as to problem area, and both study and practice actively consider social problems. To achieve this maturity, the current differences in perspectives of marketing must be synthesized.

Three such perspectives have been identified by the author—that of the manager, the critic, and the academic. Each perspective differs from the other in respect to several dimensions, yet the differences may be exaggerated and the underlying complementarity overlooked. As an instrument of social change, marketing requires all three perspectives, but not in their present divisive fashion. A call for increased communication between proponents of the three views is made with suggestions on specific ways of reaching one another. |
| Tucker (1974) | Marketing theory needs to broaden its perspective and research human resources and well-being. | The "broadened" and "generic" concepts of marketing in expanding the domain of marketing have retained the perspective of the marketer viewing the public as target markets. This development has taken place despite the fundamental differences between business and nonbusiness activities or the unrealized expectations of increased welfare. Marketing theory must change its focus in the future. Instead of analyzing the consumer, focus should be on human resources; instead of researching choice of brand A or brand B, theory should concern itself with the relationship between consumption and human well-being. The labor market and consumer behavior (from the view of consumer's *own* well-being) are two areas |

CHAPTER TWO

Marketing:
A Social System
Perspective

INTRODUCTION

In recent years there has been considerable interest and concern about the nature of marketing.[1] This is accounted for by many factors, such as the overall maturing of the discipline, more and better research capability, greater consciousness of marketing practice, increased interaction with sister disciplines in the social sciences, and recognition by diverse groups of the vital role of marketing in society. A perspective on marketing is offered here which differs from those expressed by other writers, although it does not necessarily contradict or exclude them. The perspective put forth builds upon social exchange theory which is consistent with, and indeed central to, current definitions of marketing and is also consistent with essential marketing phenomena.

This chapter begins with a discussion noting some of the ways in which marketing can be viewed as a social system, and two examples of one particular perspective, the buyer-seller perspective, are presented. Next, the basic notion of exchange suggested by Wroe Alderson is presented briefly. Following this is a more extended discussion of social exchange propositions put forth by George C. Homans. Each proposition is followed by a brief marketing illustration. There then follows an extended discussion of how the basic

---

[1]Richard J. Lewis and Leo G. Erickson, "Marketing Functions and Marketing Systems: A Synthesis," *Journal of Marketing,* 33 (July 1969), 10-14; Philip Kotler and Sidney J. Levy, "Broadening the Concept of Marketing," *Journal of Marketing,* 33 (January 1969), 10-15; Donald P. Robin, "Toward a Normative Science in Marketing," *Journal of Marketing,* 34 (October 1970), 73-76; Philip Kotler and Gerald Zaltman, "Social Marketing: An Approach to Planned Social Change," *Journal of Marketing,* 35 (July 1971), 3-12; Philip Kotler, "A Generic Concept of Marketing," *Journal of Marketing,* 36 (April 1972), 46-54; Daniel J. Sweeney, "Marketing: Management Technology or Social Process?" *Journal of Marketing,* 36 (October 1972), 3-10; Ben M. Enis, "Deepening the Concept of Marketing," *Journal of Marketing,* 37 (October 1973), 57-62; Jerome B. Kernan, "Marketing's Coming of Age," *Journal of Marketing,* 37 (October 1973), 34-41; W. T. Tucker, "Future Directions in Marketing Theory," *Journal of Marketing,* 38 (April 1974), 30-35.

concepts in these propositions can be used to construct a conceptual foundation of marketing as an exchange-based social system. Each of Homans's propositions is recast in a marketing context and presented as a marketing proposition. A single illustration or control is used to operationalize these propositions. The propositions are interrelated and presented in paradigm form. There is also a discussion of liaison variables that affect the dynamics of the process described in the paradigm. Some of the implications of a social system perspective are treated. This chapter concludes with a discussion of social systems as marketing.

MARKETING AS A SOCIAL SYSTEM

Marketing can be viewed, somewhat radically perhaps, as a social system. A *social system* is (1) a set of interrelated people or groups, (2) engaged in reaching a shared goal, and (3) having patterned relationships with one another. Implicit in this view is a definition of *marketing* as *the process in which exchanges occur among persons and social groups.* This process is a dynamic one in which widely heterogeneous forces interact in ways that participants or observers may evaluate either positively or negatively.

There are several social system perspectives that can be used based on the definition of a social system given above. Other perspectives could involve the marketing profession as a social system, or marketing departments and marketing consulting or research agencies as social systems. Viewing the *profession* as a system of interacting individuals involves a sociology of knowledge and a sociology of the profession's approach to the study of marketing. These approaches would look at marketing as a macrosocial system having recruiting and training institutions as well as other maintenance institutions, such as the American Marketing Association and research and consulting agencies; ritual interactions, such as formal meetings; other formal channels of communication, such as its journals, and so forth. Marketing as an *organizational component* is a microsocial system within a firm where individuals having specific marketing tasks, such as research, brand management, and sales force management, interact in specified ways to achieve common goals. This perspective involves a sociology of formal organizations approach. A third perspective is to consider as a social system marketing entities in *vertical* (wholesaler-retailer) and *horizontal* (retail trade associations) relationships to one another. These approaches and many others are all valid ways of looking at the very complex phenomenon of marketing.

In this discussion, however, attention will focus on a fourth more familiar social system, that created by *buyer-seller interaction.* This social system perspective, particularly when using exchange theory, has not been developed in marketing despite its centrality in contemporary definitions of marketing. One word of caution: even though the words *buyer* and *seller* may be used in the singular, the reader should remember that buyers interact with other

buyers and sellers interact with other sellers in ways that affect the relationship of a single buyer and a single seller in any given interaction. In fact,
opinion leadership, reference group theory, competition, and so forth, are
widely studied marketing forces emerging from the highly complex situation
where all parties—sellers and buyers—interact directly or indirectly with
each other.

As an initial example consider an early form of a conventional marketing
context, the bazaar, which is still a prevalent mode of marketing in many
areas of the world. (A variant of this in developed nations is the flea market.)
A woman seeking food items visits a bazaar or marketplace in which the selling locations of particular goods and services are grouped together. In this
case, there is a physical structure relating to the social structure and, as we
shall see, this may also influence the exchange process. The *physical structure is provided by the grouping together* of all vendors and within this larger
group the clustering of vendors of identical goods (e.g., tomatoes, bread, and
so forth) or services (e.g., barbers or blacksmiths). Buyers and sellers will
also share with their comparable role occupants and to a more limited degree
with one another certain values and norms which help create a social structure. The buyer and the seller share a common goal—the consummation of
an exchange: the buyer wanting as much bread as he can obtain while giving
up as little money as possible, and the seller wanting as much money as he
can obtain while giving up as little bread as possible. For this goal to be
achieved, there must be an interaction of buyer and seller—a relationship
must be established. This relationship will be operationalized initially as an
exchange of communication—both verbal and nonverbal—and perhaps later
as a physical exchange as money and bread are swapped. Objectively viewed,
the buyer is selling money in return for bread while the seller is buying money
by giving up bread. It matters little that one commodity (money) is a generalized medium of exchange while the other (bread) is specific. There is an inherent conflict in that each party wants to get as much as possible while
giving up as little as possible. However, both are motivated to consummate
an exchange. This motivation increases the likelihood that the conflict will be
resolved. Behavior in markets or bazaars is remarkably similar whether the
location is El Salvador, Afghanistan, or Bangladesh. Each party will feign a
lack of real interest in bringing about an exchange. The person selling money
will criticize the quality or the amount of bread he or she is being offered for
purchase while the party buying money through selling bread will scorn the
small quantity of money offered. Gradually, adjustments are made in the
terms of trade, expressed interest increases, each party becomes a little more
facilitative, and a transaction occurs. The presence of other buyers and
sellers as third parties has an important impact on the exchange relationship.
The bread vendor knows that others, in all likelihood in adjoining stalls, are
offering the same commodity and that the money vendor can try his or her
luck with them and in fact will if at some point the cost of the transaction is
too high in terms of the dollars that have to be supplied or the time necessary

to negotiate or the quantity or quality of bread being forgone relative to initial expectations. Similarly, the money vendor seeking bread knows that many other people are seeking the same commodity, and the bread vendor may prefer to invest his marketing efforts in those other sources of money.

For the person who thinks this situation does not characterize contemporary marketing practice in highly developed societies, a visit to an automobile showroom or a used-car lot is suggested. First, in approaching the location of a new- or used-car dealer, the potential customer is likely to notice other dealers in the same neighborhood, a reminder that some comparison shopping is relatively easy in terms of accessibility of alternative sources for an automobile. The customer will be approached quite quickly by a salesman upon entering the car lot or showroom. Once a particular automobile has been identified, the negotiation begins. The astute buyer will quote one price and the salesman will counter with another, but usually only after a third party, the sales manager, has been consulted. The insistent bargainer will claim that the price is too high and may threaten to leave by actually standing up or putting his coat on in preparation to go. The salesman, who typically represents himself as being on the customer's side in the negotiation (and may even display some hostility concerning the sales manager), will generally then ask for another counteroffer (perhaps himself suggesting a specific price) to bring to the sales manager. The customer may accept the price and insist that it represents the absolute maximum. The salesman visits the manager, who generally remains out of view, and likely as not returns with an approval. The buyer knows that there is a price below which the dealer will not go and hopes he can reach it, and the salesman hopes to do better than that. Recognizing a good or knowledgeable customer, he may identify this bottom price clearly and early.

THE BASIC NOTION OF EXCHANGE

Alderson characterized transactions, or the "Law of Exchange," as follows:

> Given that x is an element of the assortment A_1, and y is an element of the assortment A_2, x is exchangeable for y if, and only if, these three conditions hold:
>
> (a) x is different from y
> (b) The potency of the assortment A_1 is increased by dropping x and adding y
> (c) The potency of the assortment A_2 is increased by adding x and dropping y.[2]

We can restate Alderson's law as follows: Given that money (x) is among the resources (A_1) a buyer has, and that clothing (y) is part of the resources

---

[2]Wroe Alderson, *Dynamic Marketing Behavior* (Homewood, Ill.: Richard D. Irwin, Inc., 1965), p. 84.

(A_2) a department store has, money is exchangeable for clothing if, and only if (1) money differs from clothing (generally speaking, we would not swap $10 of our cash for $10 of someone else's cash), (2) the clothing being added to the buyer's resources makes him happier than he would have been had he held on to his cash and acquired no additional clothing, and (3) the department store feels itself better off overall by giving up the clothing and taking the cash.

In the section that follows, several propositions suggested by George Homans will be presented and eleborated in a conventional marketing setting. While the elaborations could be made highly complex, parsimony is more in order. The intent is to develop an exchange theory or model of marketing as a social system. While the buyer-seller social system is used, a comparable exchange model could be developed for the other social system perspectives of marketing mentioned earlier.

SOCIAL EXCHANGE PROPOSITIONS
APPLIED TO MARKETING

The propositions discussed in this section are based on the work of George C. Homans. Each of these propositions is operationalized in a conventional marketing-related context. The propositions involve the concepts of reward frequency, reward value, critical mass of rewards, reward-punishment discrepancy, stimuli similarity, and approving behavior.

Proposition I.   *For all actions taken by persons, the more often a particular action of a person is rewarded, the more likely the person is to perform that action.* [3]

Of all consumer actions, the particular actions most often providing satisfaction are the actions most likely to be repeated. For example, if, of all leisure time activities, movie going is most likely to be rewarding, that is, the incidence of bad movie pictures being relatively less than the incidence of, say, bad picnics, the more likely consumers will be to attend movies rather than picnics. Similarly, if a consumer in his purchase of appliances finds that particular brands of appliances are better than others, he will be more likely to buy those brands again.

Proposition II.   *If in the past the occurrence of a particular stimulus, or set of stimuli, has been the occasion on which a person's action has been rewarded, then the more similar the present stimuli are to the past ones, the more likely the person is to perform the action, or some similar action, now.* [4]

[3]George C. Homans, *Social Behavior: Its Elementary Forms*, rev. ed. (New York: Harcourt Brace Jovanovich, 1974), p. 16.

[4]*Ibid.*

Proposition I emphasized the importance of rewards. Stimuli are another important dimension, although many psychologists argue that rewards themselves are stimuli. The corresponding marketing proposition would be that other things (such as objective product quality) being equal, when a buyer associates a past rewarding interaction with a particular type of salesman, he is more likely to be receptive to other salesmen of the same type. Product characteristics, advertising, and other marketing variables could readily be substituted for *salesmen.*

Proposition III.   *The more valuable to a person is the result of his action, the more likely he is to perform the action.*[5]

The higher the magnitude of a reward accruing to buyers from certain actions, the more likely they are to repeat those actions. Correspondingly, the greater the punishment or dissatisfaction a consumer associates with a particular action, the less likely he is to repeat that action. Thus not only will a consumer buy a particular brand of salad dressing more frequently than others because to him it is superior to others, but the more he likes that brand, the more of it he will consume. Similarly, the more a buyer likes a salesman, the greater the interaction with that salesman and presumably the more he will purchase from that salesman.

Proposition IV.   Deprivation-Satiation Proposition. *The more often in the recent past a person has received a particular reward, the less valuable any further unit of that reward becomes for him.*[6]

This proposition raises the issue of whether a particular reward is valued differently on different occasions depending on the recency of its last occurrence. Thus the more recently a person has visited a theater relative to another pending visit, the less valuable that pending visit will be. Of course, the notion of a critical threshold is of great importance. The greater the number of theater productions attended in the recent past, the more likely this principle is to operate, but it may require a rather specific minimum number of "recent past" visits before the principle becomes operative. The principle of satiation in psychology and the law of diminishing returns in economics are similar ideas.

Proposition Va.   Frustration Aggression. *When a person's action does not receive the reward he expected, or receives punishment he did not expect, he will be angry; he becomes more likely to perform aggressive behavior, and the results of such behavior become more valuable to him.*[7]

[5]*Ibid.*
[6]*Ibid.*
[7]*Ibid.,* p. 37.

Consider an instance where the quality of the interaction of salesman and buyer was the key factor in the purchase of a product. Furthermore, assume the product fell decidedly short of expected performance. The buyer is punished in two ways: his product expectations were violated, and the interaction with the salesman becomes retroactively disappointing and of lesser quality and hence an additional loss or punishment is inflicted. In all likelihood the buyer generalized from a high-quality interaction with the salesman to a (imputed) high-quality product. Product disappointment is then generalized backward to disappointment with the salesman. Thus the customer is likely to be less receptive or even hostile to that particular salesman or others like him. Also, unfavorable experiences with one brand of a product may result in aggression operationalized in the form of nonpurchase of other products under the same family brand name, or they could result in negative word-of-mouth communication. For reasons consistent with good social-psychological theory (not eleborated here), this hostility may itself be rewarding to the buyer.

Proposition Vb. *When a person's action receives the reward he expected, especially a greater reward than he expected, or does not receive punishment he expected, he will be pleased; he becomes more likely to perform approving behavior, and the results of such behavior become more valuable to him.* [8]

When a buyer finds a product innovation to be better than expected during a trial period, he is much more likely to adopt the innovation (approving behavior) which in turn is more valuable to him on a full scale than he had projected it to be prior to the trial period. If a salesman is involved, approving behavior may manifest itself in terms of not just an adoption but in terms of referrals of other potential adopters to him. That referral activity itself may be rewarding to the buyer to the extent that others follow or imitate his behavior and adopt the innovation. In some cases, a threshold effect may occur with too much reward. Guilt or dissonance may result when one is given more than he expected or at least feels is deserved.

CONCEPTUAL FOUNDATIONS FOR VIEWING MARKETING AS A SOCIAL SYSTEM

Let us now look at these basic premises—or, in Homans's terms, propositions—as they provide a foundation through their interconnectedness for the view of marketing as a social system. There are essentially seven concepts or variables providing the fundamental structure of relationship: (1) frequency of reward (punishment), (2) likelihood of action, (3) similarity of stimuli, (4) value of the reward, (5) recency of last critical mass of the rewards, (6) discrepancy of expected reward (punishment) with reward (punishment) real-

[8]*Ibid.,* p. 39.

ized, and (7) degree of approving (disapproving) behavior. In principle, these variables are all interrelated, forming twenty-eight two-variable propositions without expression of direction of causality. We shall examine one particular interaction among these variables which describes the exchange process between a buyer and a seller. Each party in the exchange process has his own particular perspective of that social interaction.

For the buyer, *the recency of the last critical mass* for a type of reward, say the benefits of a vacation, is sufficiently dated so that any satiation effects will have worn off. Vacations for this person (unlike those for the so-called workaholic) are *frequently rewarding* when taken. Moreover, a particular type of vacation, say a two-week stay in a small resort town, has been found to be more highly rewarding (the value dimension) than other vacation options. Furthermore, it may be that the last such vacation was arranged by a travel agent who developed a vacation plan that considerably *exceeded the buyer's expectations* (discrepancy between actual and expected reward). The *likely action* of the buyer is that he will reward the travel agent by again engaging his services (approving behavior). Another likely action is that the buyer will express a preference for the same or similar type of vacation (*stimuli similarity*).

There is a similar structure of relationships for the travel agent. Past experience suggests that certain types of clients "fit" well into certain vacation plans and that the client in question is *similar to persons* (*stimuli similarity*) who enjoyed one particular plan, which was the plan suggested for and used by the client. The reward for the travel agent is the repeat patronage and referrals by clients. Thus the matching of client types (and the attending research and record keeping) with particular vacation plans is the *frequently rewarded* activity for the agent. Apart from the financial consequences, there may be professional pride or satisfaction derived as well. It is known that working with a repeat client is a greater source of job satisfaction for the travel agent than working with a new client, so that the reward-repeat patronage is also a more *highly valued* allocation of his efforts. After a period of time has passed since the last contact with a client about his vacation plans (*recency of last reward* for the travel agent), he will often contact (*likelihood of action*) the client with information about various vacation plans. Depending on the client's response, there may or may not be a *discrepancy between expected and actual rewards.* If the travel agent expects a two-week vacation request and the client expresses an interest in a three-week vacation, a favorable discrepancy exists (a more-expensive vacation implies more money or approval for the agent). The agent will, in all likelihood, express *approving behavior* for such action to encourage the financially more attractive (to the travel agent) three-week plan. Approving behavior may take the form of indicating that the three weeks the buyer had in mind is indeed a more optimal period of time to spend on the type of vacation the client desires.

It is important to note in the above examples the very strong degree of interdependence of travel agent and client. Each is the object and recipient of

FIGURE 2-1

Core Exchange Variables Defining the
State of Buyer-Seller Interaction

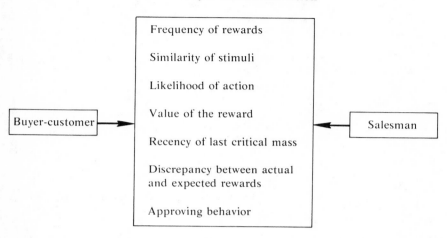

the other's approval behavior which is a source of reward. Each is sensitive to the recency of last reward (vacation plan sold on the one hand and vacation plan consumed on the other hand) and the appropriateness or timeliness of a renewed contact and that the frequency of the interaction is a partial function of the positive or negative incongruence between expected and actual rewards.

Thus important concepts affecting the exchange patterns between buyer and seller can be presented as in Figure 2-1. Using these variables, a set of marketing specific propositions can be put forth which collectively constitute a theory of social exchange in marketing.

Marketing
Proposition I: The recency of the last critical mass of reward for the buyer is inversely related to the likelihood of a purchase (sale):

• • •

Marketing
Proposition II: The greater the realized reward relative to expectation, the more likely a buyer (salesman) is to respond in the future to identical or highly similar salesmen (buyers):

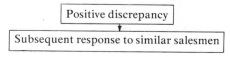

• • •

Marketing
Proposition III: Given positive discrepancy (better product performance,
easier sale) and similar stimuli (salesmen or buyers), approving behavior is likely to be expressed which in turn increases
the likelihood of a purchase (sale):

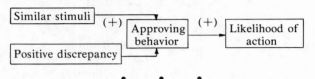

•   •   •

Marketing
Proposition IV: The greater the frequency of reward a consumer receives, the
more likely he is to favor similar stimuli associated with that
reward:

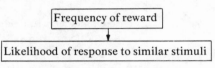

•   •   •

Marketing
Proposition V: The greater the frequency of reward, the more likely it is that
a critical mass exists, thereby decreasing the likelihood of a
subsequent purchase:

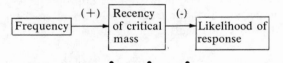

•   •   •

Marketing
Proposition VI: The greater the value of the reward, the less the importance
of recency of last critical mass as an inhibitor of action and
the less important frequency of reward is in increasing the
likelihood of a purchase:

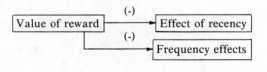

•   •   •

Marketing
Proposition VII: The greater the value of a reward received by a buyer, the
stronger the approving behavior displayed:

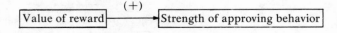

There are, of course, many additional relationships that could be stated. Figure 2-2 is a schematization of the seven propositions. Because it does not present all possible relationships, it is only a partial indication of a foundation for viewing marketing as a social system. Mutual or reciprocal causation and interaction effects are undoubtedly present. It is to be stressed that each variable in Figure 2-2 involves a behavioral and/or a psychological interaction of a buyer and a salesman. It is this interaction and resulting relationship that constitutes the core of the marketing social system.

As indicated, Figure 2-2 is a simplified core structure of relationships within the social system created by the interaction of the individual buyer and the firm where the latter is often represented in the form of salesmen, advertising, catalogs, corporate images, products, and so forth.

LIAISON VARIABLES

What must now be added to Figure 2-2 is the set of variables that gives social character to the various relationships. Consider the norm of reciprocity as a key variable operating within, that is, guiding and structuring, the core social system. The norm of reciprocity refers to the sense of obligation one develops toward another as that other party is perceived to be investing his valuable resources in oneself. Thus a salesman is perceived by a customer to be investing in that customer time which could be spent in other valuable ways, such as with other customers, and the more this time exceeds customer expectations, the greater the feeling of obligation the customer feels and hence the greater his desire to show approving behaviors. The astute salesman will want to create or enhance this sense of obligation. The sense of obligation could be discharged by making a purchase. The social norm is supported by or participated in by the customer as a result of a psychological feeling of obligation which in turn could result in part from the socialization process begun early in life in the larger social system. Thus to the extent that a norm of reciprocity exists in the marketing social system, the functioning of concepts in the core system in Figure 2-2, such as approving behavior, are affected.

Still other sociological phenomena add important dimensions. Consider the concepts of interpersonal homophily and heterophily. There are almost an infinite number of traits in which persons may differ or correspond. For example, social homophily may affect the functioning of the stimulus similarity and reward value core exchange variables. Broadly speaking, social class is important in determining the nature of communication between buyer and seller. More importantly still, social class and those variables that it encompasses, such as education, income, and occupation, affect what commodities are assigned relative values and the magnitude of those values. Social class also affects feelings about the recency of critical mass. An even-

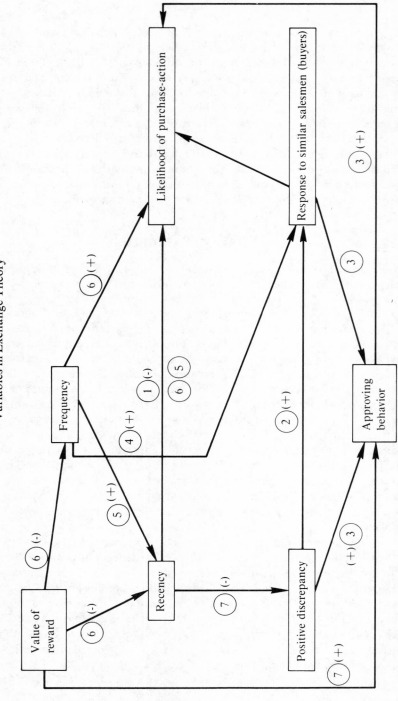

FIGURE 2-2

Possible Relationships Among Key
Variables in Exchange Theory

Circles numbers refer to corresponding marketing proposition number.

ing of expensive entertainment may have greater value for a low-income consumer than for a high-income consumer and be less likely to contribute significantly toward the creation of a critical mass of such leisure time activity. Differences in the ability to pay for such entertainment are, of course, the critical intervening variable. Note that we are not referring to identical forms of entertainment, but simply to the cost. (The low-income consumer may feel uncomfortable in the entertainment spots frequented by high-income consumers.)

In summary, the view of marketing as a social system, using as an example that aspect of the system involving direct interaction of two conventional roles, buyer and seller, can be presented as in Figure 2-3. Buyers and sellers bring certain traits and circumstances to the exchange situation which affect the rewards or the punishments exchanged. Liaison variables moderate the exchange process, as discussed briefly in the examples above. Figure 2-3 provides the foundation for numerous propositions, many of which can be interrelated to form theories.

FIGURE 2-3

Marketing as a Social System:
Buyer-Seller Interaction

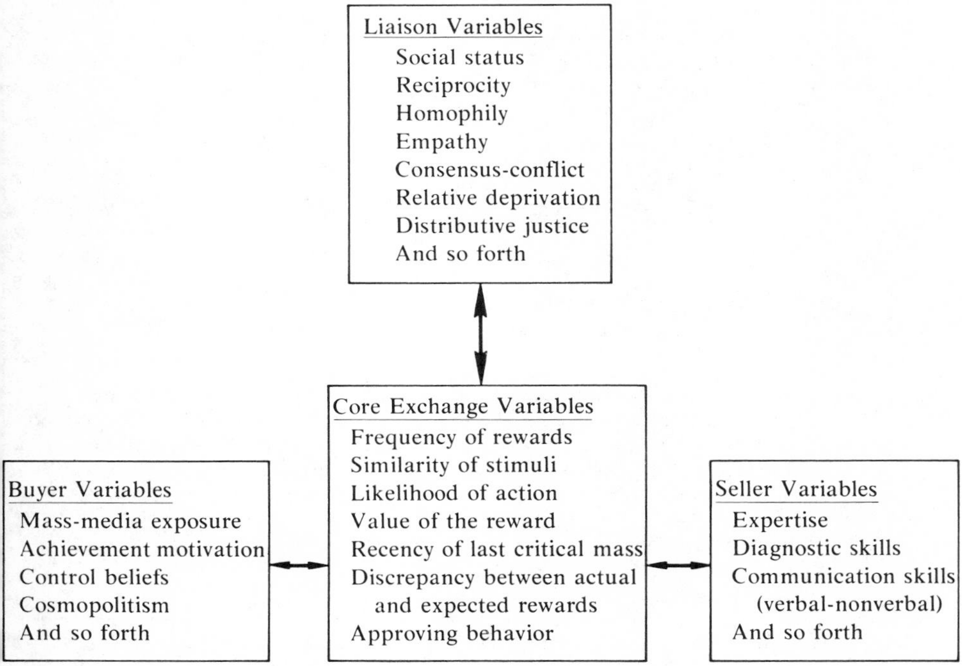

Liaison Variables
    Social status
    Reciprocity
    Homophily
    Empathy
    Consensus-conflict
    Relative deprivation
    Distributive justice
    And so forth

Core Exchange Variables
    Frequency of rewards
    Similarity of stimuli
    Likelihood of action
    Value of the reward
    Recency of last critical mass
    Discrepancy between actual
        and expected rewards
    Approving behavior

Buyer Variables
    Mass-media exposure
    Achievement motivation
    Control beliefs
    Cosmopolitism
    And so forth

Seller Variables
    Expertise
    Diagnostic skills
    Communication skills
    (verbal-nonverbal)
    And so forth

TABLE 2-1
Power Bases in the Buyer-Seller Dyad

Seller	*Buyer*
Legitimate Power Bases	Legitimate Power Bases
(a) reputation of company	(a) authority for latitude in
(b) reputation of individual	purchasing decisions
(c) authority for latitude in	
terms, i.e., price setting,	
delivery schedules	
Expert Power Bases	Expert Power Bases
(a) degree of product knowl-	(a) degree of knowledge about
ledge—own and competitor	seller's products and com-
	petitive products
(b) degree of knowledge about	(b) degree of knowledge about
buyer company needs and	buying, companies' needs,
problems	and decision processes in their
	determination
Reward Power Bases	Reward Power Bases
(a) offering favorable terms	(a) purchase
(b) offering information about	(b) offering information about
pending pricing/inventory/	future company buying plans
shipping/product changes in	(c) offering worthwhile leads to
seller's company	the seller
(c) offering information about	(d) offering entertainment or
competitors of the seller	services to personally bene-
(d) offering entertainment or	fit the seller
services to personally	
benefit the buyer	
Referent Power Bases	Referent Power Bases
(a) degree of similarity to buyer	(a) degree of similarity to buyer
on actual personal character-	on actual personal character-
istics of perceived importance	istics of perceived importance
to buyer	to seller
(b) successful interpersonal tech-	(b) successful interpersonal tech-
niques of ingratiation	niques of ingratiation
Coercive Power Bases	Coercive Power Bases
(a) threat of increased delays or	(a) threat of withdrawing busi-
increased price on needed	ness completely from seller
future supplies from seller	(b) threat of reducing quantity
(b) threat of quality problems	ordered or unwillingness to
at prices below those stated	accept past terms of seller
by seller	
(c) threat of insufficient supply	
and high demand for a good	
buyer is interested in	

Source: S. W. Bither and P. S. Busch, "Social Power: A Perspective for Viewing the Buyer-Seller Dyad in Industrial Marketing," Working Paper 17 (University Park: Pennsylvania State University, 1972).

Bither and Busch have analyzed the buyer-seller dyad in industrial marketing in terms of social power which is implicit in much of the discussion above. Tables 2-1 and 2-2 summarize their perspective which is a very promising approach to understanding the marketing social system established by interacting parties. The reader should treat the information in Tables 2-1 and 2-2 as hypotheses in need of testing.

TABLE 2-2

The Domain of Social Power

Market Situation: *Competitive Distinctiveness*	*Effect of Social Power* *on Outcome*
Seller's product and terms are highly differentiated from competitive offerings and match buyer's needs exactly	outcome* depends little on the effective use of social power unless a competing seller can effectively exert coercive power over buyer
Seller's product and terms are undifferentiated from competitor's offerings	outcome depends completely on the effective use of social power by both buyer and seller
Seller's product and terms are slightly differentiated from competitor's offerings and slightly inferior in terms of buyer's needs	outcome depends largely on the effective use of social power by both parties
Seller's product and terms are highly differentiated from competitor's offerings and distinctly inferior in terms of buyer's needs	outcome depends little on the effective use of social power unless seller can effectively exert coercive power over buyer

Source: S. W. Bither and P. S. Busch, "Social Power: A Perspective for Viewing the Buyer-Seller Dyad in Industrial Marketing," Working Paper 17 (University Park: Pennsylvania State University, 1972).

*Outcome is defined as the probability of a sale accomplished between the buyer and seller in the situation depicted.

IMPLICATIONS

The introduction to this chapter argued that the marketing profession can be viewed as a social system or as a number of social systems, depending on the particular viewpoint assumed. One implication of this is that each way of viewing marketing as a social system can produce new insights. The sociology of knowledge and the sociology of professions were mentioned as substantive areas having information that could increase insight into the marketing world, although this chapter does not elaborate upon this possibility. However, a better sociological understanding of marketing as a knowledge-producing and action-oriented profession would undoubtedly reveal areas where the profession could be improved and could probably suggest specific remedial action to be undertaken by appropriate professional agents or organizations. The social system perspective selected for development concerned the buyer-seller system. Using exchange theory, a few dynamics of the processes and phenomena of *relationships* between buyer and seller were discussed. The value of this approach is that it helps identify specific variables and relationships between variables which the practitioner can either manipulate or adapt to other factors to create harmony with an essentially unalterable other factor. Thus the salesman or possibly the product manager may want to improve the financial or psychological value of his product the more recently the last purchase of the product occurred. Or the sales manager may decide to train salesmen to identify and use the norm of reciprocity where it exists to elicit approving behavior in the form of sales.

Viewing marketing as a social system can therefore be of benefit to the profession itself in terms of its overall performance and to the individual marketer in his dealings with departmental colleagues and the consumer.

SOCIAL SYSTEMS AS MARKETING

At the center of the controversy of what marketing is lies the question of domain. In this section of the chapter we would like to present the notion that social systems such as families, friendship groups, business organizations, and churches are also marketing phenomena. While conventional marketing situations can be considered in social system terms, social systems can be considered in conventional marketing terms. By keeping marketing connected with the exchange of goods and money, it remains more clearly a matter of applied economics. The rhetoric of seller and buyer is sustained; profit is the seller's goal and economic purchase the buyer's. One source of enlargement in marketing thinking is the desire to explain seller and buyer behavior ever more fully or precisely for the sake of more inventive selling action or more accurate prediction of outcomes. Then it is only reasonable to want to know more about the motives of the participants in the marketplace, requiring more study of human motives as they affect purchase decisions: psychology is needed, and by extension (potentially) all knowledge of the culture and the groups within it.

This basic logic underlies most contemporary theories of marketing behavior and was summed up by Wroe Alderson in his statement that "every phase of marketing can be understood as human behavior within the framework of some operating system."[9] The operating system he has in mind is the one involving "the double search in which customers are looking for goods and suppliers are looking for customers . . . a joint decision in which

[9]Wroe Alderson, *Marketing Behavior and Executive Action* (Homewood, Ill.: Richard D. Irwin, Inc., 1957), p. 1.

the customer agrees to take the goods offered and the supplier agrees to sell at the stated price and terms." [10]

Similarly, Bartels discusses a general theory of marketing, offering a broad view but retaining the traditional boundaries implied by references to consumption, distributive systems, and institutions technically differentiated for economic purposes:

> A contemporary general theory of marketing is implicit in a sufficiently broad concept of marketing . . .
>
> Marketing is —
>   the process
>   whereby society,
>   to supply its consumption needs,
>   evolves distributive systems
>   composed of participants, who,
>   interacting under constraints —
>   technical (economic) and
>   ethical (social) —
>   creates the transactions or flows
>   which resolve market separations
>   and result in exchange and consumption. [11]

Bartels's position has been sharply criticized at a metatheoretical level by Shelby Hunt. [12]

The early endeavors to carry out research on marketing behavior as having psychological and sociological wellsprings (as well as economic) were termed *motivation research*. Rather rapidly they moved beyond the boundaries of traditional categorization to note that not only was marketing behavior a subset of human behavior, as Alderson said, but that the behavior of non-business entities was also marketing behavior. At the Eighty-fifth Annual Forum of the National Conference on Social Welfare, Levy pointed out this widening use of marketing research:

> Non-commercial organizations, both governmental and private, also became concerned with their "market," whether that market be patients for physicians and dentists (so that professional organizations sponsor research), or financial contributors (in which case a charitable body may commission a study), or citizens or volunteers or voters (in which case the government or political parties may be interested in research). [13]

---

[10]*Ibid.*, p. 75.

[11]Robert Bartels, "The General Theory of Marketing," *Journal of Marketing,* 32 (January 1968), 32.

[12]Shelby Hunt, "The Morphology of Theory and the General Theory of Marketing," *Journal of Marketing,* 35 (April 1971).

[13]Sidney J. Levy, "Motivation Research," *Community Organization 1958* (New York: Columbia University Press, 1958), p. 129.

This view was subsequently elaborated in later articles on broadening the concept of marketing to indicate its application in public, nonprofit, and quasi-private spheres.[14] In pressing toward defining the root character of marketing in business and other contexts, one emphasis has been on the nature of exchange. Since some kind of exchange is involved in all human interactions, they are potentially susceptible to a marketing analysis. Customarily, this analysis is couched in positive terms. Alderson's marketing system is one in which suppliers and customers are "looking for" each other and make a "joint decision" in which each "agrees" to sell or take. Similarly, Kotler offers marketing as "the set of human activities directed at facilitating and consummating exchanges." [15]

More basically, marketing is what people do when they want to provide something to, or get something from, someone else. Because the kinds of things offered or sought vary, as do the time, place, and participants, it is possible to distinguish many categories of marketing. For example, the providing or getting that goes on between people in their private lives, where the content of the exchanges that occur are such as parental attention, filial devotion, sexual gratification, reprimanding, and teasing, may be termed *intimate marketing.*[16] This category is a matter of analytic perspective. Analyzed by a religious person, marriage is a sacrament; by a political scientist, it may be viewed as a power struggle or a unit with a particular sort of voting pattern; and a lawyer may note if the marriage is legally contracted. A marketing analysis would ask what each member of the marriage offers, provides, gives—in traditional parlance, "sells"—and what each member wants in return, whether interpreted as a price or as that which he "buys." From this point of view it is not foolish or demeaning to analyze the marriage in terms of the services the wife provides as cleaner, cook, lover, mother, and so forth, the worth of those services to the husband, their market value if offered elsewhere, and what she wants or gets in return. She is providing a type of labor. A common complaint is that married men dislike paying the price of saying "I love you," and in consequence, many marital deals fall through.

Intimate marketing is no less marketing for seeming relatively primitive when its makeup is compared with that of the major *commercial marketing* systems with their elaborated networks of communications, transportation,

[14]Kotler and Levy, *op. cit.;* Sidney J. Levy and Philip Kotler, "Beyond Marketing: The Furthering Concept," *California Management Review,* 12 (Winter 1969),67—73; and Gerald Zaltman and Brian Sternthal, eds., *Broadening the Concept of Consumer Behavior* (Chicago: The Association for Consumer Research, 1975).

[15]Philip Kotler, *Marketing Management: Analysis, Planning and Control* (Englewood Cliffs, N.J.: Prentice-Hall, Inc., 1972), p. 12.

[16]For a fuller discussion of this, see Zanvel Klein and Gerald Zaltman, "My Body, Our Decision: Husband-Wife Decision Making in Surgical Contraception," in Zaltman and Sternthal, *op. cit.*

and product development. Similarly, susceptible of marketing analysis are the aims, actions, and interactions that occur in the spheres variously delineated as *nonprofit marketing,* conducted by various social agencies, the social marketing of prosocial goods and ideas,[17] political marketing of candidates and political positions, and so forth.[18]

The assertion of the omnipresent character of marketing considerations in human relationships—their pervasiveness in the social system—is a source of discomfort to various thinkers. Much confusion is introduced into marketing study by the widespread tendency to equate the whole of marketing with certain of its components. For example, it is customary to think of hard-sell salesmen, deceptive advertising, shoddy products, inefficient delivery, and improper prices as being of the essence of marketing. Even friends of marketing find it difficult to resist accepting the disparaging rhetoric of marketing critics. For example, a professor of marketing administration, discussing marketing theory in the *Journal of Marketing,* showed apparent agreement with Edgar Friedenberg, who criticized educators for resembling advertising agencies in efforts to learn "what the customers are really like, and more willing to adapt its appeals to their actual motives and life styles," and thus to exploit their motives.[19] He went along with Charles Silberman, who opposed "gimmickry and packaging" to "substantive change," with the implication that a generic view of marketing would support the former but not the latter. The implication is that a good marketer would not be concerned about trying to have a good product, meaning one that was beneficial to its users. Also cited are Erik Erikson, Erich Fromm, and others who are critical of people acting as consumers in their personal lives, who have a "marketing personality." Some of the confusion here comes from the fact that while all people market themselves if they are to have reciprocal relationships, certain of their presentations are more valued by the personal and social critics than are others, so that to offer strong and able selves, to be spontaneous and creative, are not seen as being "offerings," but are of a kind they value, whereas ingratiation, marked adaptation to the desires of others, and being an ardent consumer, and so forth, are signs of the marketing orientation.

The radical (and simple) definition of marketing as giving and getting, providing and receiving, extends in several directions. It comprises endless units for analysis by virtue of referring to the individual and his status of developing and preparing his offering and his relative inclination to receive; dyadic, face-to-face exchanges; individuals vis-à-vis social units, agencies, enterprises; and such organizations facing each other. The definition is im-

---

[17]Kotler and Zaltman, *op. cit.*

[18]Avraham Shama, "Candidate Image and Voter Preference: A Theory and Experiment" (doctoral dissertation, Northwestern University, 1973).

[19]W. T. Tucker, "Future Directions in Marketing Theory," *Journal of Marketing,* 38 (April 1974), 30-35.

partial to the actor, and any element or interaction may become a unit of study—contrary to the custom of most text books, which focus on the sellers' viewpoints. [20] The goal is to look in both directions or in as many directions as there are participants, not to assist one in "exploiting" another (except as readership has that effect), but to examine how they come to provide and to take that which they do.

Given this fundamental view, that marketing is a discipline that can examine all exchange systems for what is exchanged, and the various attendant circumstances and processes, the social system can be approached as a marketing system. Warner and Lunt had something of this basic idea in mind when they pointed out that the social regulation of the behavior of man consists of "(1) a division of labor necessary for manipulating tools in acquiring a living from nature, and (2) a distribution of the newly formed desirable goods. The type of social organization possessed by a group will determine the allocation of pleasant and unpleasant tasks among its members as well as the sharing of the spoils . . ." [21]

As a concluding note we should add that viewing social systems as marketing phenomena requires broader interpretations or logical extensions of many terms. For example, the concept of profit must be broadened beyond its usual operationalization in terms of money. Profit may be represented by increments in learning, added longevity, lessened anxiety, and so forth.

[20] Philip Kotler and Sidney J. Levy, "Buying Is Marketing Too!" *Journal of Marketing,* 37 (January 1973), 54-59.

[21] W. Lloyd Warner and Paul S. Lunt, *The Social Life of a Modern Community* (New Haven, Conn.: Yale University Press, 1941), p. 24.

CHAPTER THREE

Marketing as
a Cause and Consequence
of Change

INTRODUCTION

The present rate of social change in most parts of the world is unparalleled in the history of man. In many societies this change is taking place exponentially, and marketing is playing a key role in this change process. This association between marketing and social change is a dynamic one. Marketing activities are a causal force in social change and a consequence of social change as well. More strongly, marketing is the *instrument* of much social change.

The role of marketing as a contributory force in social change and particularly in nonprofit situations is currently receiving considerable attention from marketing, social planners, and others. The first formal, systematic expression of this appeared in an article by Philip Kotler and Gerald Zaltman in which the term *social marketing* was introduced. Social marketing was defined as *"the design, implementation, and control of programs calculated to influence the acceptability of social ideas and involving considerations of product planning, pricing, communication, distribution, and marketing research."* [1] This definition is primarily concerned with the use of marketing inputs. A broader perspective is provided by Lazer and Kelley, who define social marketing as *"that branch of marketing concerned both with the uses of marketing knowledge, concepts, and techniques to enhance social ends as well as with the social consequences of marketing policies, decisions, and actions"* [2] (italics added). Lazer and Kelley broaden the definition provided by Kotler and Zaltman to include topical areas usually referred to as consumerism, marketing and society, and so forth, which imply account-

---

[1] Philip Kotler and Gerald Zaltman, "Social Marketing: An Approach to Planned Social Change," *Journal of Marketing,* 35 (July 1971), p. 5.

[2] William Lazer and Eugene Kelley, *Social Marketing: Perspectives and Viewpoints* (Homewood, Ill.: Richard D. Irwin, Inc., 1973), p. 4.

ability and responsibility for the consequences of marketing activity in non-profit settings. Whether the term social marketing should be broadened to encompass consequences of a marketing input into a social program is an interesting issue for debate, but this is beyond the scope of this discussion.

As increasing attention is being given to social marketing as an approach to planned social change, it is appropriate that we not lose sight of the role of "plain," or conventional, marketing in social change. A better awareness and understanding of the relationship between marketing (in the conventional sense of the word) and social change can help marketers to realize their full potential as a positive force in the process of social change.

AN OVERVIEW OF SOCIAL CHANGE

It is generally contended that a change in wants is the starting point of social change in any given social system.[3] The change in wants may be experienced initially or most strongly by someone outside the system in which change is to be introduced. Securing the advocated change in the target system is the means by which that want is satisfied. When someone outside the target system attempts to satisfy his wants by manipulating some facet of the target system, we have a case of proactive external intervention.

Social change in a system does not always or necessarily require an external agent. Pressure for change may originate among the leaders of a society who direct change efforts downward, or pressure for change may originate at more of a grass-roots level with change efforts being directed upward toward the leadership. Rogers (1973) refers to these as top-down change and bottom-up change.[4] He suggests the following propositions:

1. "Power elites act as gatekeepers to prevent restructuring innovations from entering a social system, while favoring functioning innovations that do not immediately threaten to change the system's structure." [p. 81]

2. "Top-down change in a system, which is initiated by the power elites, is more likely to succeed than is bottom-up change." [p. 83]

3. "Bottom-up change involves a greater degree of conflict than top-down change." [p. 83]

4. "Bottom-up change is more likely to be successful at times of perceived crises in a system." [p. 84]

5. "Bottom-up change is more likely to be successful when a social movement is headed by a charismatic leader." [p. 85]

6. "The role of the charismatic leader in a social movement decreases as the movement becomes institutionalized into a more highly structured organization." [p. 85]

[3]Figure 3-1 is a paradigm of the discussion in this section.

[4]Everett M. Rogers, "Social Structure and Social Change," in *Processes and Phenomena of Social Change,* Gerald Zaltman, ed. (New York: Wiley Interscience, 1973), pp. 75-88.

FIGURE 3-1

Selected Change Phenomena Prior to
the Adoption-Rejection Phases

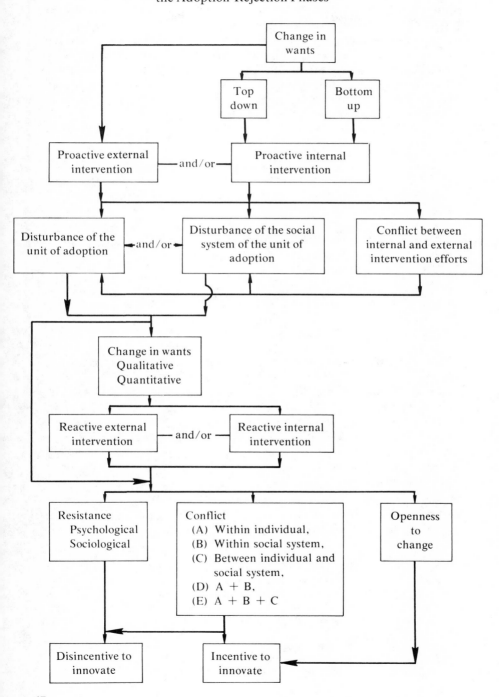

When efforts at want satisfaction arise within a social system to satisfy wants experienced by (some) members of that system, we have an instance of proactive internal intervention. Proactive internal intervention and proactive external intervention may occur together. However, certain special conditions may arise. External and internal change agents (at top or bottom) may have identical wants that they wish to satisfy but may differ in the means they select for intervention. Alternatively, external and internal change agents may employ similar or identical modes of intervention to satisfy different and perhaps conflicting wants. The possibilities are as follow:

TABLE 3-1

Types of Social Change

| | | *Internal and External Change Agents Have:* | |
		Shared Modes of Intervention	*Different Modes of Intervention*
Internal and External Change Agents Have:	*Shared Wants*	Total consensus	Intervention dissensus
	Different Wants	Want dissensus	Independent change programs

It should be noted at this point that a change in wants is assumed as a condition for the precipitation of social change. A changed want may go totally or partially unsatisfied or may be satisfied in an undesirable way for a protracted time period. This may give the appearance that a change in wants never occurred. It is contended here that even current but "old" wants that are connected with social change did at some point in time involve a change. The change could have been qualitative in that it was a new want or quantitative in terms of the intensity with which it was or is experienced.

Coleman (1973) points out that the major division between theories of planned change is between those that take as their starting point changes in the individual and those that take as their starting point changes in social conditions surrounding the individual:

> This distinction is one that pervades nearly all action programs designed to produce change. One approach is based on the premise that if only the material conditions in which a group or society finds itself are changed, then the group or society will itself go ahead to expand its resources. An opposing approach is based on the premise that if only the individuals themselves are changed, then they will move toward an expansion of resources. [5]

[5]James S. Coleman, "Conflicting Theories of Social Change" in *Processes and Phenomena of Social Change,* Gerald Zaltman, ed. (New York: Wiley Interscience, 1973), p. 62.

It therefore seems advisable to distinguish between change efforts directed toward the specific individual or group one is trying to alter and change efforts directed toward the larger social system or environment in which the target individual or group exists. Change efforts can of course be directed toward both levels at the same time. In general, this might well be the most appropriate approach. It is possible, however, that conflict between internal and external intervention efforts may occur and that this conflict may have a special disturbing effect on the unit of adoption or on the larger social system. The effect of the conflict may be functional or dysfunctional to the initial change effort.

In the instance of planned change, the intended effect of the disturbance created by the initial (proactive) intervention is to produce a change in wants. Again, the alteration may be of two sorts. In the first instance there may be a cultivation of new wants. Such qualitative changes at least with regard to basic wants are unlikely in the short run, and it is the short run that is usually of greater concern to marketers. Alternatively, the impact of the intervention may be to make more salient—more obvious and more strongly experienced—already existing wants that are not being satisfied or are being met but by an alternative that has undesirable side effects or dysfunctional consequences.

The response to the new or improved opportunity to respond to a change in wants is termed reactive. It must be within the set of conditions associated with the wants, however much those conditions were affected by the proactive intervention. Once again, the changes in wants may have occurred at some point in time well prior to the reactive intervention. Also, the changes in wants leading to reactive intervention may in no way be connected with an instance of proactive intervention. Reactive intervention may be both internal and external in origin, with perhaps one occurring after the other has proved itself ineffective.

Intervention, particularly reactive intervention with its heavier orientation toward attitudinal and/or behavioral commitment to some particular idea, practice, or thing, may encounter resistance and/or conflict and/or openness to change. The net effect of these forces is to provide either an incentive or a disincentive to innovate.

AN EXCURSUS ON WANTS

Considerable mention of wants has been made above. As indicated earlier, theorists argue that alterations in wants are the starting points of social change and that the manner in which they are satisfied provides any individual society with its uniqueness or distinct quality. A discussion of these concepts and their corresponding marketing phenomena is in order. Marketing in very conventional ways responds to various wants, with goods and services affecting not only the material aspects of society but the nonmaterial aspects as well. Stated somewhat differently, the presence of wants is a necessary, but not sufficient, condition for change. However, the existence of these wants plus their satisfaction through marketing activities constitutes the necessary and sufficient condition—or ingredients—for social change in a wide number of areas in social life. The nature of some wants and marketing's involvement with them is discussed below.

There are many types of wants. First there are wants that reflect the desire to receive recognition and distinction. Many instances of innovativeness and opinion leadership, concepts of central importance for new-product marketing, can be explained by the existence of *credit wants*. Innovators seek "credit" or recognition by being pioneers. Opinion leaders receive part of their gratification by having others seek their advice and part by the resulting imitation. The relevance of these wants varies according to context: (1) Not all new ideas receive a warm public reaction. The use of marijuana and consciousness-expanding drugs are cases in point. (2) Many innovations occur without thought of credit on the part of the originators. For example, the introduction of air conditioning in a neighborhood is probably influenced more by interpersonal processes than by the desire for credit. (3) Some people will disavow any credit for an idea or action if it turns out to be bad. Few like to admit to being a former Edsel owner. In this case, the act of buying the Edsel was an innovative one with very little consequent imitation.

Next are wants that ease tension when satisfied. Examples are impulsive acts and general random activity. Gum chewing, smoking, and so forth are supposed to be means of easing tension. Convenience goods and impulse products are purportedly purchased because of the desire or want to reduce tension.

Another type of wants relates to the individual's need for self-presentation and self-definition. These wants influence the way we structure and organize our perception of the environment and are most likely to express themselves in products such as automobiles, in preference for different architectural forms, and so forth. The popularity of Scandinavian-design furniture may reflect certain styles of life, such as casual living. Preferences for particular architectural forms are considered to reflect one's own definition of self. Prefab-housing design is initially based on market surveys of self-definition among representative consumers.

Some wants are linked with other wants; the nature of the linkage or connection between wants produces a certain degree of tension which, if it is to be reduced, requires a novel solution. In this case, wants of different origins converge on a single product which may be an innovation. Some multipurpose products, such as a compound pain-reliever, are examples.

Some wants arise when satisfaction of an original desire is blocked. In this case, an alternative desire (end) may be adopted. In addition, when one avenue for satisfying a desire is blocked, an alternative means may be adopted. An example is the popularity among weight watchers of the low-calorie beverages and the nondairy, dairylike products. The use of low-calorie products is an alternative to lowering the intake of soft drinks, and so forth.

Some wants emerge as a result of satisfying other wants. For instance, levels of aspiration may increase as a result of increased education (the original want). The insurance industry is largely based upon these wants. When the want of acquisition or ownership is satisfied, a new need or want develops. This is the want of security or protection, which is afforded by the insurance industry. In fact, this industry can be viable only in a highly owner-ship-oriented society.

There are three other types of wants. Creative wants emphasize accomplishment for its own sake. The act of creation is more important than is the thing created. While do-it-yourself products are sold because they generally result in useful things and savings, part of the motivation to buy them is that the process of using them is also satisfying. Relief and avoidance wants are another category. A new household product may be desired to relieve boredom or it may be desired to save time, thus allowing the housewife freedom to pursue goals new to her. Quantitative variation wants are not concerned with quantitative variation per se but with qualitative changes in things that permit or result in quantitative changes. Having more is not the issue so much as having something different that enables you to have more. Thus some innovations come into being because they alter quantitative boundaries. New labor-saving devices are developed because housewives want more free time. Installment credit plans tend to result in larger sales volumes and greater store loyalty. New products or behavior are thus linked with the desire to conserve effort, space, and material. Birth-control programs are an important example of attempts to vary the population size and growth.

THE EXCHANGE PROCESS IN MARKETING AS SOCIAL CHANGE

The relationships between social structure, social functions, social exchange, and marketing are summarized schematically in Figure 3-2. These relationships are discussed below.

Social change is the process by which alteration occurs in the structure or functioning of a social system. Social structures such as distribution systems build up, in part, around interacting individuals. Social interactions, best described as a social exchange process, serve many purposes—some of which are basic to the existence of a society. *Social exchange* is the process whereby two or more parties supply benefits (or penalties) to one another for mutual gain (or loss). It is the core mechanism for social life. Among the more important *functions* of social exchange are control of disruptive behavior, socialization, sharing of goals and orientations, regulation of means of

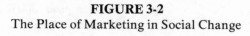

FIGURE 3-2
The Place of Marketing in Social Change

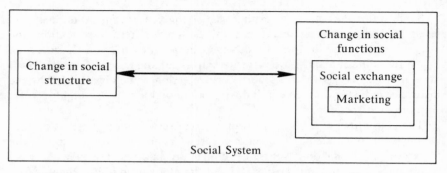

achieving goals, role differentiation and role assignment, communication, and establishing adequate relationships with the environment. The nature of social structures is derived from the character of interpersonal or exchange relationships, and, conversely, social structures also affect the exchange process. Thus there is an interaction of structure and function in social life such that a change in one creates tension for change in the other.

Any set of human activities affecting exchange relations is of crucial importance. Regarded from this perspective, marketing is the body of thought and action addressed to exchanges, becomes a major motor force in society and in social change in particular. Marketing, then, is concerned with understanding the various factors that help bring about social exchange and with using this understanding to stimulate selected social exchanges.

A full understanding of social exchange-related factors involves an orientation toward the other party or parties in the exchange process. The idea of being oriented toward and sensitive to the other party's needs and circumstances as a way of improving the frequency and magnitude of exchange has been termed the *marketing concept,* as has been discussed. Marketing management, on the other hand, is the process of using information gained by such an orientation to analyze, plan, implement, and control the exchange process by relying on such tools and working concepts as product, price, promotion, and place.

The exchange process is a major mechanism enabling society to function. Marketing management, then, technically speaking, engages in social change when it attempts to alter ongoing exchange relationships or to bring about a new exchange relationship. Marketing management also engages in social change when it attempts to act directly on structural variables in order to create circumstances for a better exchange relationship or when it indirectly causes structural change by altering an exchange process which in turn affects social structure. In a more practical sense, it is likely that some threshold or degree of alteration has to be reached before significant social change can be said to have occurred. In developmental economics this has been termed the "takeoff" point. The same phenomenon occurs with minor events as well. Up to a certain point there may be strong, widespread resistance to a new product, but once this point has been passed there may be a dramatic reversal. Large numbers of people initially resisting the new product rapidly come to adopt it. This is commonly displayed graphically by S-shaped cumulative adoption curves describing the diffusion of innovations. When several such events occur in the same sector of social life their summation can add up to impressive change, although when these events are viewed singly there may be difficulty discerning any social change.

MARKETING AS CAUSE AND CONSEQUENCE

Wittingly or unwittingly, marketing, and by implication marketing management activities, are sometimes causes and at other times consequences of social change. Marketing, when done in response to a change in social conditions, helps shape society's reaction to changed social conditions. Marketing as a cause of social change helps determine the areas in which social change will occur. Causes and consequences are frequently in a multiple serial relationship to one another: cause A produces consequence A, which in turn becomes cause B producing consequence B, and so forth. The classic example of this is Henry Ford's motorcar. A general increase in discretionary income helped create conditions supporting a market for automobiles. This new buying power, together with improvement in the technology of mass production which made it profitable to produce a car, resulted in a market. The buying power created a latent market, and the availability of the cars converted the latent market into a real or manifest market. The very existence of this psychologically and socially attractive product stimulated in potential adopters a desire for ownership and the willingness to save the necessary funds for purchase. The desire to realize more profit stimulated further development in the technology of mass production. The resulting savings in manufacturing costs kept automobile prices from increasing or at least from increasing faster than discretionary income. Figure 3-3 is a schematic portrayal of this process.

The relationships between cells in Figure 3-3 need some additional observations. Cells 4 and 5 in Period 3 are, in effect, new cells 1 and 2, constituting a new "Period 1" for the same market or a new market. Thus cell 6 in Period 4 is essentially cell 3 in Period 2 for the same or a new market in a subsequent time period. The new "Period 2" situation, for example, could involve changes in the residential distribution of some population. In the United States the overall improvement in transportation eventually, along with other important factors, facilitated movement to the suburbs, which resulted in a decentralization and consequent proliferation of retail outlets and their grouping in shopping centers. Shopping centers, in turn, increased the

FIGURE 3-3

The Process Demand Stimulation

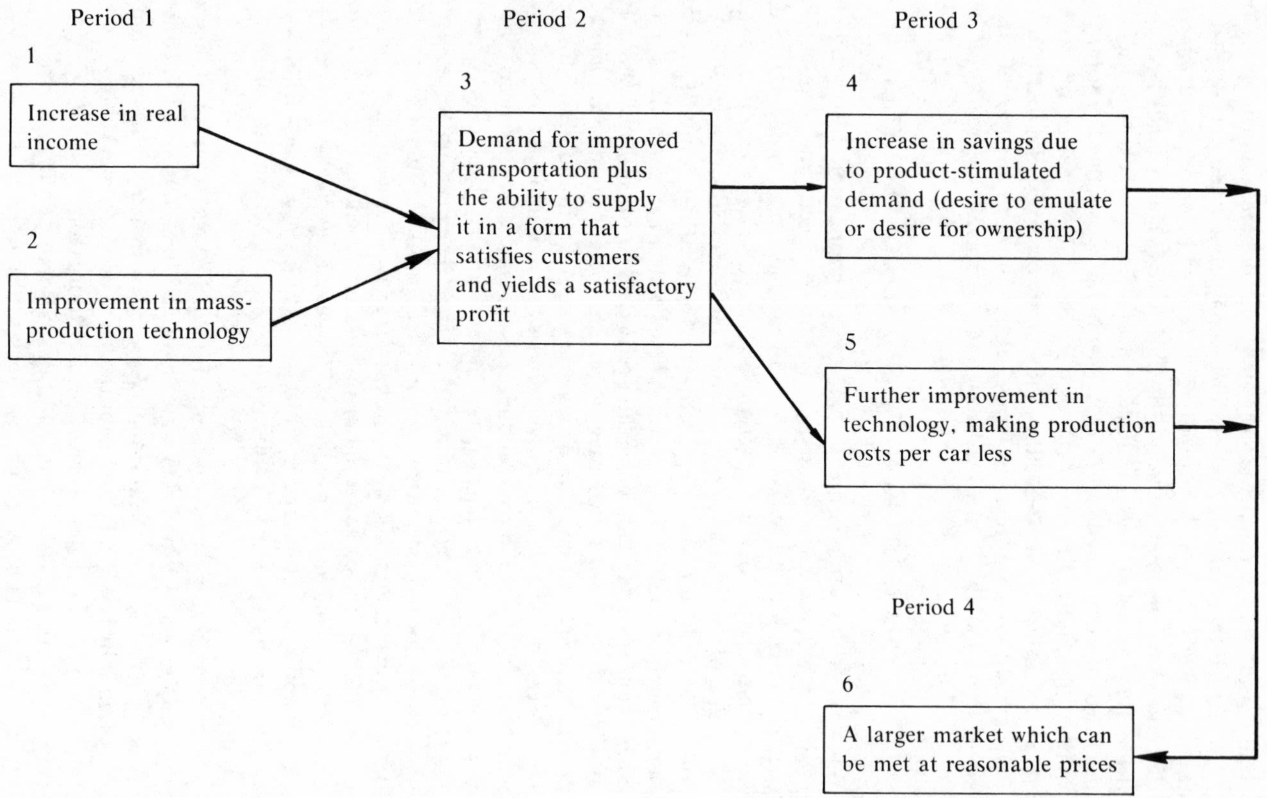

Period 1

1
Increase in real income

2
Improvement in mass-production technology

Period 2

3
Demand for improved transportation plus the ability to supply it in a form that satisfies customers and yields a satisfactory profit

Period 3

4
Increase in savings due to product-stimulated demand (desire to emulate or desire for ownership)

5
Further improvement in technology, making production costs per car less

Period 4

6
A larger market which can be met at reasonable prices

attractiveness of suburban living, which helped maintain or even increase residential (and occupational) movement from the city to the suburbs. Many nonmarketing factors are obviously involved in all these events. However, in the absence of marketing management's response to the changing social conditions, the events described would probably not have occurred.

The transistor radio is another example of how a change in one social sector, in this case technology, produces a marketing opportunity resulting in social change in another social sector. Many Latin-American health workers credit the transistor radio, particularly the inexpensive Japanese brands, as one of the major tools in national development. Health educators in Costa Rica, for instance, are now able to reach most families in rural areas with special messages about family planning, nutrition, and general child care. These messages, whose diffusion is possible primarily because of the widespread ownership of transistors, are causing major changes in the quality of life for many rural families. Qualitative changes of life in rural areas are beginning to create new marketing opportunities in these regions.

TYPES OF SOCIAL CHANGE

It will be useful to take another perspective on the role of marketing in social change. Six types of social change have been suggested, using time and societal levels as basic dimensions (see Table 3-1). Type 1 refers to attitude

TABLE 3-1

Types of Social Change

	Level of Society		
Time Dimension	*Micro (individual)*	*Intermediate (group)*	*Macro (society)*
Short term	Type 1 1. Attitude change 2. Behavior change	Type 3 1. Normative change 2. Administrative change	Type 5 1. Invention-innovation 2. Revolution
Long term	Type 2 Life-cycle change	Type 4 Organizational change	Type 6 Sociocultural evolution

change and behavior change. For several reasons, attitude change does not always result in corresponding behavioral change: (1) normal opportunities may be missing to express attitudes through overt behavior; (2) certain artificial barriers prevent behavioral change in response to a change in attitudes; (3) attitudes may change but not be strong enough to produce a change in behavior; and (4) attitudes other than those changed may be involved but are inconsistent with the desired behavioral change. There are many other reasons as well relating to methodological problems and philosophy of science issues. Also, behavioral change does not necessarily imply attitude change. Basically, however, much marketing effort is devoted to changing attitudes or behavior. Advertising and product differentiation are among the most common marketing techniques. The addition of color to condoms is credited with the increased usage of condoms among persons not previously using any form of contraception. Persons active in this area believe this product differentiation through color has changed basic attitudes and behavior. Thus one brand of condoms exhorts people to "embark on a new adventure with this exotic prophylactic in South Sea color. . . ." Consumers can adventure with "sunset red," "midnight black," "dawn pink," "morning blue," or "siesta green."

Marketing is both a cause and a consequence of Type 2 change. Marketers respond to consumer demands unique to each stage in the life cycle, and as the number of consumers in each stage varies so does the volume of marketing activity associated with each stage vary. To the extent that marketers control the exact form of products available to satisfy needs associated with different life-cycle stages, marketers also influence the manifestations of consumer behavior at those stages. There is an increasing demand for planned retirement communities which is channeling construction and real estate activity in this direction. It has been observed that, as in other contexts, the physical planning of these communities greatly influences the frequency of interaction of residents as well as their leisure life style. Differently designed communities are producing different experiences for people entering this new period of their lives.

Type 3 change involves alterations in group norms, values, and membership. According to one report the energy crisis, a major marketing phenomenon, indirectly resulted in the formation of new social cliques. Apparently people who ride together stay together. Car pools, where none had existed before, led to new friendships, which in turn led to social gatherings for entertainment purposes only. The longevity of such social cliques (like that of the car pools) may be questionable, but their existence was very real at the time of the report. Changes in group norms and values and the attendant "drug culture" have proved to be an uneradicable stimulant to elaborate, imaginative underworld processing and distribution systems. Contrary to popular wisdom, values can change significantly in relative strength within short periods of time. Rokeach suggests that within a recent three-year period several values in the United States have become significantly more important: a world at peace, a world of beauty, equality, mature love, being logical, and loving. Significantly less important values were a comfortable life, a sense of accomplishment, family security, social recognition, and being clean.[6] These changes in values are already reflecting themselves in marketing activities both by *conventional* marketers and by persons and groups not traditionally viewed as marketers.

Changes in norms and values, for example, may ultimately reflect themselves in organizational change with alterations in existing organizations or the development of new organizations. This is Type 4 change. Many for-profit organizations have appeared in the last few years, appealing to the middle-aged divorced or widowed group, apparently in response to greater stress on such values as mature love and loving. The lessening of the importance of family security (a lessening in importance of a product of the family as a marketing system) may be a contributor to the increased supply of divorced persons to whom such agencies as "Parents without Partners" appeal. The stress on equality has been stimulated as well as reinforced by vigorous marketing by women's liberation groups.

Invention and revolution, Type 5 change, can produce rapid large scale social change. Military establishments viewed as marketing social systems are active producers of political change. In one country in Central America, the military is also using its vast logistical system and network of military personnel to distribute and sell contraceptives throughout that country. As indicated earlier in the chapter, the automobile and mail-order merchandising have had major and relatively quick impacts on society as both cause and consequence of social change. The pharmaceutical industry, through its research and development and marketing activities, has had a nearly incalculable effect on the demographic structure and quality of life in many societies or particular groups within societies. The marketing of and by political candidates has been effective in contributing to the passage of major legislation. Lobbyists obviously play a key role in this process. As conservationists are quick to point out, many commercial marketing-related activities may possibly have rapid and significant deleterious ecological effects, and they market their ideas to offset these.

Type 6 social change involves the long-term ramifications of any of the preceding types of change. The consequences of the transistor radio and the automobile for national development have already been cited. The impact of contraceptive technology developed and disseminated by commercial agencies on female occupational behavior has been tremendous, leading to a change in the composition of the work force, which in turn through demonstrating opportunities for significant employment by women (and despite continuing sex discrimination) leads to greater demand for contraceptives.

[6]Milton Rokeach, "Change and Stability in America—Value Systems, 1968-1971," *Public Opinion Quarterly*. 38 (Summer 1974), 222-38.

COMMENTARY ON SOCIAL MARKETING

The concept of social marketing as the application of marketing technology and processes to furthering social change has been introduced in an earlier chapter. This chapter will conclude with a brief commentary on social marketing and an extensive example. First it must be stressed again that so-called marketing techniques are not unique to marketing. Persons and groups in nonconventional marketing situations also utilize many marketing processes and techniques. The main consideration the reader might have in mind is that such persons or groups would perform their tasks better if they were more fully aware of how these processes could be engaged in more fruitfully and the techniques applied more precisely. This requires greater knowledge of the traditional marketing area where these processes and techniques have been most highly developed. Also, many ideas in conventional marketing can be used to gain a broader perspective on social change problems. For example, many basic marketing strategies can be used to stimulate strategic questions for planned social change. The following outline uses two areas where social change is needed and is taking place to illustrate how broader perspectives on social change may be obtained through the explicit, systematic use of conventional marketing ideas.

Marketing Strategies and Communication-Related and Nutrition-Related Social Marketing Questions

I. *Market Penetration*

A. Basic Strategy: Improve the company's position with its present products in its current markets.

B. Marketing Question: What should be done to gain further acceptance of existing products?

C. Social Marketing Questions:

1. Do the data indicate which appeals may stimulate more mothers in rural areas to practice family planning?

2. How can we get more mothers in rural areas to use protein-enriched flour?

II. *Market Development*

A. Basic Strategy: Find new classes of customers that can use the company's present products.

B. Marketing Question: What new users are there for the present product line?

C. Social Marketing Questions:

1. Do the data indicate who else (what other market segments) present advertising should be directed to without a change in copy?

2. Should we direct our promotional efforts concerning protein-enriched flour to low-income families in urban areas in addition to those in rural areas?

III. *Reformulation Strategy*

   A. Basic Strategy: Improve present products to increase sales to current customers.

   B. Marketing Question: What product changes are suggested?

   C. Social Marketing Questions:

   1. Do the data identify promotional themes that should be altered to attract more attention from the present target audience?

   2. Can the taste and texture of the protein-enriched flour be improved to make it more appealing to mothers in rural areas?

IV. *Market Extension Strategy*

   A. Basic Strategy: Reach new classes of customers by modifying present products.

   B. Marketing Question: What changes in goods and services are necessary to reach nonusers?

   C. Social Marketing Questions:

   1. What additional mass-media channels do the data indicate as necessary to reach discontinuers or resisters?

   2. Can taste and texture be changed to appeal to mothers in low-income urban areas?

V. *Replacement Strategy*

   A. Basic Strategy: Replace current products with new improved products.

   B. Marketing Question: What should replace present products?

   C. Social Marketing Questions:

   1. Do the data suggest alternative substitute appeals or themes?

   2. Should vitamins be added to the product?

VI. *Market Segmentation—Product Differentiation Strategy*

   A. Basic Strategy: Attract new customers by expanding the assortments of existing product lines.

   B. Marketing Question: Should products be modified to appeal to different groups of buyers or users?

   C. Social Marketing Questions:

   1. Do the data indicate that different types of appeals should be used simultaneously to attract different groups of family-planning adopters?

   2. Should different types of enriched flour be used to appeal to different groups, e.g., vitamin-enriched flour to some groups and protein-enriched flour to other groups?

VII. *Product Line Extension Strategy*

   A. Basic Strategy: Add more products based on the same technology.

   B. Marketing Question: Should more goods and services be made available to current consumers?

   C. Social Marketing Questions:

   1. Do the data indicate that the advertising or communications mix should refer to ideas other than family planning?

   2. Should enriched soft drinks be distributed *in addition* to enriched flour to rural mothers?

VIII. *Concentric Diversification Strategy*

    A. Basic Strategy: Attract new customers by adding products that have synergistic effects with the present line.

    B. Marketing Question: Are there new products suggested by the research that will attract consumers who will also start buying existing items in the product line?

    C. Social Marketing Questions:

        1. Do the data suggest or identify appeals or themes associated with nonfamily planning services that would enhance the impact of family-planning appeals (i.e., would have a positive interaction effect when placed together in the same basic communication effort)?

        2. Can the introduction of enriched soft drinks in rural areas lead in turn to greater use of enriched flour in these areas?

IX. *Forward-Backward Integration Strategy*

    A. Basic Strategy: Improve efficiency by directing efforts to activities prior to, or following, current efforts.

    B. Marketing Question: What opportunities exist for vertical expansion of the company's activities?

    C. Social Marketing Questions:

        1. Are there appeals in messages to ultimate users of contraceptives that may also be effective in motivating field workers, informal community leaders, and so forth?

        2. Should the manufacturer of enriched flour expand its activities to include the distribution of the product?

The furtherance of social ideas through more explicit use of marketing may be undertaken by business-oriented or nonbusiness-oriented persons and groups. In either the business or the nonbusiness instance, the basic phenomenon is social in nature. Many health-related agencies, for example, have a specific job classification for marketing-planning or marketing-programming directors.

A good example of marketing in action in an underdeveloped country is the Sri Lanka Social Marketing Project's use of commercial resources to promote and distribute the concept and practice of family planning. Involved in this effort is Population Services International, the Family Planning Federation of Sri Lanka, the International Planned Parenthood Federation, and the government of Sri Lanka (Ceylon), all nonprofit agencies.

Based on research on contraceptive usage in India, it was determined that complete coverage of the target population would require annual sales of 200,000,000 condoms. One percent of this number (two million) was chosen as a reasonable sales goal for the first year. It was also decided to aim for a total of 4,000 retail outlets for the condoms by the end of the first year. This number would represent 10 percent of the 40,000 retail stores—grocery shops, eating houses, pharmacies, etc.—in Sri Lanka that were considered to be possible outlets for the condoms.

Use of Market Research

The starting point in any marketing campaign is to survey the potential consumers and retailers in order to learn: their likes and dislikes, the degree to which they already use or stock similar products, and what their attitudes are toward the product. On the basis of this kind of information, the following can be determined: the right place to sell the product, the right way to promote it, and the right price. Typically, such information is gathered by a market research company.

In Sri Lanka, PSI hired the Lever Brothers Research Division to carry out the market research which included: surveys of the public's knowledge, attitudes, and practices regarding family planning, with special reference to condoms; a product survey among the public and potential retailers to determine preferences regarding distribution methods, names for the new product, size and color of packaging, and pricing; the present stocking practices of retailers; and their knowledge and attitudes regarding family planning, particularly condoms.

PSI learned the following facts from these surveys:

- Awareness and approval of family planning is high;
- Detailed knowledge of family planning is often incomplete;
- Use of reliable family planning methods is low;
- People want their sources of family planning supplies to be as convenient as possible;
- Only one-half of one percent of the retailers were stocking condoms;
- People want to be able to buy small numbers of condoms at a time;
- A price of 10 to 15 rupee cents (approximately U.S.$0.01) per condom is considered an acceptable retail price by both retailers and the public.

Role of the Advertising Agency

The critical problem of creating demand through thoughtful promotion of the product was turned over to the De Alwis Advertising Company, an experienced local agency. Its first task was to create different prototype packaging, brand names, and symbols or logos for the product, which were then tested during the market research described above.

The advertising agency recommended that the image developed for the new brand of condoms should be as positive as possible. One name they suggested and the one ultimately chosen for the product on the basis of a market survey was *Preethi,* which means "joy" in the two major languages spoken in Sri Lanka. *Preethi* thus conveys an image that is the opposite of that generally associated with condoms (for example, the belief that condoms inhibit the man's sexual pleasure). The advertising agency wanted a symbol or logo that would also be positive as well as functional. The logo chosen was based on the well-known circular shape made with the thumb and forefinger that means "good" or "OK." It is functional in the sense that a shy customer can ask for *preethi* condoms by using this symbol rather than having to say the name outloud.

The basic messages, developed by the advertising agency on the basis of the results of the market research, appear in all of the media being used for the campaign. *Preethi* is promoted as the trusted way to plan one's family: *"Preethi* is simple, safe, sure." The campaign revolves around the theme that "the planned family is a happy family." A typical press ad, which shows a father clasping a child protectively, reads as follows:

> Until you want another child rely on *Preethi*—a trusted way to plan your family. Everyone today talks frankly about planning families. Millions of people all over the world are spacing out the birth of their children. By doing so each child gets more attention, more food and a better education. Mother's health is greatly improved. The father has less anxiety. You too can plan your family with *Preethi. Preethi* is a safe, sure contraceptive for men. Ask for *Preethi* from your dealer. *Preethi* is specially packaged for your convenience. A packet of three costs only 40 rupee cents. *Preethi* is simple, safe, sure.

The mass media campaign has involved the use of radio, cinema, and booklets; but by far the greatest stress has been on press advertisements. The press campaign was initiated by using "teaser ads," that is, just the logo without the name or any text whatsoever. This ad appeared intensively for two weeks. It was followed by an ad that showed the logo plus the name *Preethi* in the two local languages plus English, which is the same design as appears on the consumer package. Then, as the "launch piece," the ad to promote the actual product, a brief statement was added referring to *Preethi* as a "trusted way to plan your family" and to the fact that *Preethi* could be obtained in local shops. Later, to create a pro-child image, the phrase "until you want another child" was added.

To provide the public with more in-depth information, a question and answer booklet on family planning, stressing *Preethi,* was designed by the advertising agency. A color slide shown in cinemas informs the public of the availability of this free booklet as do announcements over the radio. Entitled "How to Have Children by Plan—Not by Chance," the booklet is also sent to those who order a packet of a dozen condoms through the mail order service described below. The text of the initial version of the booklet was written in both languages as well as English; but experience has shown that this format is difficult to read and thus three separate versions are being prepared for future use.

The advertising agency also developed various "point of sales" materials, that is, items that appear in or outside each shop that stocks *Preethi* condoms. Each shop is given a metal sign to hang outside to advertise the fact that *Preethi* is for sale there. Cardboard signs, shelf strips, and two dispensers were developed for use inside shops stocking *Preethi.* One dispenser holds 40 packets of condoms and represents the basic unit for wholesale distribution. The second dispenser holds leaflets describing *Preethi* for those people who want more information before they decide to purchase.

Contrary to the general expectation that such an intensive campaign is very expensive, the total cost of the promotional budget for one year is only about U.S. $20,000. This figure includes the media costs as well as the advertising agency's fee.

Distribution

The distribution problem involves moving *Preethi* condoms from the docks in Colombo to the shelves of thousands of little shops all over Sri Lanka. Instead of establishing its own expensive network to do this, PSI was able to arrange for distribution through Reckitt & Colman, a leading marketer of reputable household drugs and family products. During August and September 1973, as they made their normal rounds, Reckitt & Colman salesmen handed each of their 4,000 best retailers a promotional leaflet that included a sample *Preethi* inside a paper pocket. The leaflet appealed to the retailer as someone "who is modern in outlook, a leader of opinion and concerned with the country's problems." In addition, the leaflet pointed out that he would make a profit of 33⅓ percent.

The appeal was successful: 80 percent of the retailers (3,200) agreed to carry *Preethi* when the salesmen next called on them. By the end of the year, the retailers were selling 300,000 condoms a month, which was considerably ahead of the target set at the beginning of the project.

As a supplement to the over-the-counter sales through shops, PSI is experimenting with the use of a mail order service. This alternative means of distribution is dependent for success upon the existence of a highly reliable postal service that reaches every village in the country. Two approaches are used: one simply informs the public through the press that "you can buy *Preethi* privately by post"; the other offers a free sample and an order blank. During the first month, the mail order service had generated 800 orders and nearly 5,000 requests for samples.[7]

Obviously there are many major questions concerning social marketing both in terms of its effectiveness as an avenue for social change and in terms of its impact on society. Lazer and Kelley raise several important questions which we challenge the reader to try to address:[8] Can marketing's organizational effectiveness be applied directly to social problems? Should activities be undertaken by marketing where no financial profit exists? What activities can the government perform best and which of these should remain in the domain of the public sector? How can important social markets be made economically attractive? What is the appropriate balance between economic goals and social goals for marketing management? Who should determine the weight of marketing social responsibility? What is the appropriate mix between the public and the private involvement in solving social marketing problems? What is the appropriate organizational arrangement of institutions such as education, labor, and others that will result in efficient social marketing? What changes are required in governmental regulation to optimize social marketing approaches? How can the social performance of marketing be evaluated? How much social responsibility can a marketing group endure under current market conditions? What are the appropriate short-run and long-run standards by which to evaluate marketing management with respect to social roles?

---

[7]East-West Communication Institute, "Information, Education, Communication in Population," *IEC Newsletter,* No. 17.

[8]Lazer and Kelley, *op. cit.,* pp. 11-12.

CHAPTER FOUR

Conflict and Marketing

THE INTEREST IN CONFLICT

The issue of conflict in marketing has been relatively neglected as an area of study. Primary attention has gone to the nature of conflict as it occurs among various marketing institutions and enterprises in the form of competition. It is generally recognized that these units vie for the customer's dollar. Derived from the discipline of economics, the vying is usually interpreted as economic and focuses especially on price competition. In a sense, the major polar forms of competition often are interpreted as resulting in a minimization of conflict. The model of perfect competition leaves each individual seller powerless to affect the price, and monopoly eliminates competitive prices. In between are the many gradations of marketplace interaction in which sellers seek to be effective in getting buyers by means of pricing policies and whatever other strategies they can employ.

This general view of competition is ordinarily taken for granted as the *context* within which marketing management occurs. For example, although Rathmell's text on marketing management refers frequently to competition as a constraint of marketing action and to competitive pricing, competitive conditions, and so forth, the index does not include competition as a subject.[1] McCarthy relates competition to the slope of demand curves. He distinguishes competitive advertising as that oriented to selective demand for a specific brand, and he discusses some forms of nonprice competition.[2] He also observes some of the effects of laws relating to competition and deceptive pricing, and in the 1971 edition for the first time introduces some brief material about consumerism.

[1]John M. Rathmell, *Managing the Marketing Function: Concepts, Analysis, and Application* (New York: John Wiley & Sons, Inc., 1969).

[2]Jerome McCarthy, *Basic Marketing* (Homewood, Ill.: Richard D. Irwin, Inc., 1971).

These views do not go far in recognizing and analyzing the nature of the general subject of conflict in marketing. The concern in marketing with institutional structures and with categories of functions portrays a static situation. Attempts to introduce processes in order to account for change—especially the diffusion of innovations—tend to founder on overly rapid crystallization into stages or phases where places are occupied by groups who arrive there through possession of personality characteristics or information. What produces movement through the stages is not clear.

Philip Kotler discusses growth and competitive strategies in a more vigorous manner and with greater awareness of the nuances involved in competitive strivings. He compares business with military conflict and distinguishes four kinds of adversaries, as follows:

Competitors: Those who produce the same or similar products.

Rivals: Those who produce different products but compete for the same buyer's dollars, time, or needs.

Opponents: Those who seek to impede the company's operations (may include labor unions, citizens' groups; does not necessarily include all competitors and rivals).

Enemies: Those who seek to harm or destroy the company.[3]

These distinctions, though mainly related to competition, are a beginning toward a more dynamic conception of the market. Probably the most notable thrust in marketing study that deals explicitly with conflict in the system is represented by the work of Louis W. Stern and associates on conflict in the distribution system. Stern has explored various issues related to conflict analysis and management.[4]

A focus on the whole issue of conflict is designed to provide balance to traditional approaches, not to imply that a conflict theory is a truer one than a theory of harmonious adjustment. The purpose is to perceive the basis for vitality in the marketing system. Because the marketing system *is* the social system viewed from a particular perspective, its dynamism is inherent, as Coser notes:

. . . conflict and order, disruption and integration are fundamental social processes which, though in different proportions and admixtures, are part of any conceivable social system.[5]

[3]Philip Kotler, *Marketing Management* (Englewood Cliffs, N.J.: Prentice-Hall, Inc., 1972), p. 248.

[4]Louis W. Stern, Brian Sternthal, and C. Samuel Craig, "A Parasimulation of Interorganizational Conflict," *International Journal of Group Tensions*, 3, Nos. 1—2 (1973), 68-90; see also Louis W. Stern, *et al.* in Louis W. Stern, ed., *Distribution Channels: Behavioral Dimensions* (Boston: Houghton Mifflin Company, 1969).

[5]Lewis A. Coser, Introduction to "Collective Violence and Civil Conflict," *Journal of Social Issues*, 28, No. 1 (1972), 3.

The usual emphasis on adjustment, consummation, and mutual satisfaction is one important side of the matter, but the conflict aspect needs more examination.

Interest in conflict is of course ancient and recurs at intervals as a focus for political, social, and economic theory and analysis. This recurrence is cyclic in character, paralleling historic cycles of peacefulness and disorder. In modern times the work of Georg Simmel and that of Karl Marx were landmarks of sociology and political science, Marx seeing economic class struggles producing social change, and Simmel wrestling with the problems of maintaining individuality relative to the group. [6] Freud's interpretation of "the conflict within ourselves" made it the veritable fulcrum of human personality, with the insight that neurosis

> . . . was the result of a conflict between the libido and the sexual repression . . . symptoms being equivalent to compromises in the conflict between these two mental currents. [7]

The concurrent presence of factors of conflict and disintegration in the integration of the social process was discussed by George Herbert Mead:

> There seems to be abundant opportunity for disorganization in the organization essential to the [baseball] team. This is so to a much larger degree in the economic process. There has to be distribution, markets, mediums of exchange; but within that field all kinds of competition and disorganization are possible. [8]

The upheaval of World War II, with its spur to personality study, the subsequent upsurge of new nations, and progress toward liberation among blacks, women, youth, and various kinds of social deviants, produced a fresh concern with the topic of conflict. A large social-psychological literature grew out of the effort to analyze the nature of conflict and to interpret its functional and dysfunctional character, commonly with the aim of finding ways to reduce tensions and resolve conflicts. [9]

Hodges sums up diverse sociological positions as a debate between the functionalists and the conflict sociologists. The functionalists see a quest for harmony, with social, political, and economic systems oriented toward order, consensus, and balance. Conflict sociologists are more sensitive to other forces.

---

[6]Georg Simmel, *Conflict and the Web of Group Affiliations,* trans. Kurt H. Wolff and Reinhard Bendix (New York: The Free Press, 1955).

[7]Sigmund Freud, "My Views on the Part Played by Sexuality in the Aetiology of the Neuroses," *Collected Papers* (London: Hogarth Press, 1948), I, 279.

[8]George Herbert Mead, *Mind, Self, and Society* (Chicago: University of Chicago, 1934), p. 303.

[9]Lewis A. Coser, *The Functions of Social Conflict* (New York: The Free Press, 1956).

Society, all of social life can be conceived as something in a constant state of change, instability, friction, and showdown engagements between the powerful and the powerless, the defenders of orthodoxy and those who champion new social norms, life-styles, and power alignments.10

DEFINING CONFLICT AND POWER

The present discussion does not put a fine point on a definition of marketing conflict. As Elise Boulding noted in introducing a set of papers on conflict and community in the international system, "the papers are in no sense a definitive conceptualization of conflict and accommodation in the world community but rather contributions to a rapidly growing new body of research."11 Similarly, the aim here is to draw attention to an important aspect of marketing, to encourage fuller inquiry into conflict phenomena.

Stern makes an interesting distinction between *competition* and *conflict* by contrasting indirect, object-centered, impersonal behavior in which the desired object is controlled by a third party with direct, personal, opponent-centered behavior based on incompatibility of goals, aims, or values in which the object desired is controlled by the opponent. Certainly, situations can be characterized in these ways, and it can be useful to trace out the consequences of varied aims, loci of reward, and direction of effort. It may, however, be difficult to sustain the two definitions in the face of common usage, and given that the words have different emphases rather than just a polarity. Conflict tends to refer to *the process* itself rather than to point to aims, to the fact that there is a struggle going on, whereas competition indicates something of *the kind of conflict*—that it is a contest or vying for some kind of distinction (the prize, a higher score, greater sales, etc.).

Conflict Is an Encounter of Differences. When the nature of the encounter and of the differences is specified, then its name may be determined. The names are endless, depending on where one's interest and perception are located: the kinds of conflict can be distinguished by size, intensity, means, aims, structure, participants, outcomes, and so forth. There is warfare, which implies extreme intensity of destructiveness of aim. The participants are enemies—and the war is hot or cold, depending on whether the means being used are conventional killing or states of tension, or are subtler forms of pressures. Great nuances are suggested by states of tension, skirmishes, battles, strategic moves, and the qualifications or inhibitions imposed by international laws and the observance of other civilized courtesies. Short of supreme conflicts are the array of contending possibilities—collective

10Harold M. Hodges, Jr., *Conflict and Consensus: An Introduction to Sociology* (New York: Harper & Row, Publishers, 1974), p. 13.

11Elise Boulding, "Introduction to 'Conflict and Community in the International System,'" *Journal of Social Issues,* 23, No. 1 (January 1967), 24.

violence, civil conflict, civil disobedience, boycotts, debates, honest differences of opinion, suicide, games in their whole gamut of forms, face-to-face contests, and miscellaneous negative intergroup behaviors. Conflicts can be regarded as benign when the participants' motives are approved, when the consequences turn out to be beneficial, when the damage done seems moderate or justified. Of special intrigue are the ambiguities of motivation and philosophy, the conflict of moral and ethical prescriptions, justifications, and rationales, plus the weight of righteousness they carry.

Without differences there is no activity. As differences in air temperature create wind and weather, differences in resources and in people create social, economic, and marketing activities. When there is an encounter of differences—conflict—the differences may carry differential force in moving toward their goals. When the forces are equal, the conflict is at an impasse. Impasse is not sustained because situations are in motion, and changing elements will shift the balance of forces. *Power is the capacity of an actor to move in the direction of his goal.* Most theories of exchange and conflict have to deal with a concept of power. Dahl formulated a general definition of power and sought a measure for it: A's power over B is defined as the net increase in the probability of B enacting a behavior after A has made an intervention, compared to the probability of B's enacting the behavior in the absence of A's intervention.[12] Subjectively, one (A) could feel powerful and be regarded as powerful at achieving one's aim, even if B was cooperative or if there was no way to determine what his behavior would have been without A's intervention. But subjective power is also felt to be greater when resistance is overcome.

Among the numerous distinctions made in analyzing conflict and the ways power is exerted are Rapport's three basic modes of conflict: fights, games, and debates.[13] Etzioni discusses coercive, utilitarian, and normative sanctions as exercised in organizational relationships.[14] K. E. Boulding's general theory of conflict and defense in the social order distinguishes between threat systems, exchange systems, and integrative systems.[15] Analogously, Gamson notes such resources as constraints, inducements, and persuasion for their value in influencing others.[16] Brickman emphasizes structure as a feature of conflict relationships, comparing unstructured, partially structured, and fully structured, as well as conflict over the rules of conflict situations.[17]

[12]R. A. Dahl, "The Concept of Power," *Behavioral Science,* 2 (1957), 201–18.

[13]A. Rapport, *Fights, Games and Debates* (Ann Arbor: University of Michigan, 1960).

[14]A. Etzioni, *A Comparative Analysis of Complex Organizations* (New York: The Free Press, 1961).

[15]K. E. Boulding, *Conflict and Defense: A General Theory* (New York: Harper & Row, Publishers, 1962).

[16]W. A. Gamson, *Power and Discontent* (Homewood, Ill.: Dorsey Press, 1968).

[17]P. Brickman, *Social Conflict* (Boston: D.C. Heath & Company, 1974).

Despite the different vocabularies used, most conflict theories observe a range of intensity of difference, the major means of interaction, and the kinds of understandings participants have in reaching individual or joint aims. Conflict theory takes discontent as given—as always present. While constructive aims and outcomes may be studied also, they are not emphasized to quite the degree found in exchange theory. In the work of Thibaut and Kelley,[18] of Homans,[19] and of Blau,[20] there is a strong implication that contentment *should* be the case, and analysis focuses on how to interpret and achieve a state of mutual satisfaction.

A basic marketing analysis starts with certain core ideas. Most central are the motive and the action of the buyer. The initial impulse is in someone who wants something (product or service). In his search to find or get it, he may grow it, gather it, hunt it, or make it. This fundamental activity, in which the buyer takes from the soil or the wilderness and in turn expends his time, energy, skill, and so forth, constitutes a prototypical exchange. Although calling this exchange by the name marketing is offensive to common understanding, it might be termed *archetypical marketing.* In this archetypical situation, the buyer has no other human who acts as seller, although in providing his time, energy, and skill, he himself is also a seller who lacks another human as buyer. The provider of the plants or of the kill is, however, usually perceived as a deity of some kind, a seller god who accepts prayers and other offerings as the price of a successful harvest or hunt. Then even if only in fantasy or imagination, the exchange relationship exists or is induced.

In the actual primitive situation, there are of course people with whom other marketing activities are being conducted—intimate marketing with family and friends, the barter or trade of traditional exchanges, and conventional, commercial marketing with some form of money. As soon as other people are involved, all the components of the marketing interaction are present: that which is offered, that which is desired, the location, and the telling of the nature of the exchange—contents as well as the conditions for the transaction.

From the start, there is *marketing conflict, the encounter of marketing differences.* Since several of these are occurring simultaneously, any encounter can be analyzed at various levels and with reference to various marketing components. The assumption is that conflicts have causes that are amenable to examination. As John Spiegel has pointed out with reference to various civil disorders, the conflicts almost always have quite understandable

---

[18]J. W. Thibaut and H. H. Kelley, *The Social Psychology of Groups* (New York: John Wiley and Sons, Inc., 1959).

[19]George Homans, *Social Behavior: Its Elementary Forms,* rev. ed. (New York: Harcourt, Brace & World, Inc., 1974).

[20]Peter Blau, *Exchange and Power in Social Life* (New York: John Wiley and Sons, Inc., 1964).

and rational roots: either an underprivileged group begins to demand better treatment or more power, or an established group sees the emergence of such a challenge and moves to protect its privileged position.[21] Each participant suffers *subjective conflict* in his dual role of buyer and seller; *transactional conflict* occurs between buyers and sellers; *competitive commercial conflict* goes on among traditional buyers and sellers; and *social conflict* characterizes intragroup and intergroup marketing relations.

Subjective Conflict

Subjective conflict is basically *the individual's uncertainty about his aims.* What kind of person does he want to be, how does he want to live? Such questions are basic and affect marketing actions in their inchoate infant forms and throughout life. From goals, they rapidly radiate into derived questions about means, places, and attributes of objects. When a baby seems doubtful about whether to accept the breast or a Gerber's puree, he is starting on the problems of decision making that will confront him endlessly as a consumer.

The intensity of subjective conflict may be less in a society that permits few alternatives for its members to consider. Whether to buy a car or take a vacation, to pay for education at a private school or at a public university, to buy a new tractor now or next year, to live in a commune, to wear mini or midi, and so forth are not debatable issues to most people in the world. Because of this, many jaded affluent people yearn for the simpler life they see (usually at a distance) in stable, traditional societies where social roles seem few and the need to choose is diminished. Within such societies, which are usually poor and dominated (or oppressed) by Nature, an elite, or the supernatural, the people are commonly fatalistic or apathetic.

In modern Western society the need and the desire to choose are prevalent. That there is choice and that the choices are expressive of the person are basic assumptions and basic values. Equally basic, if often less valued, are the constraints that people recognize, that decisions must be made between alternatives and one must give up something, that some alternatives are not available, that past alternatives have vanished—perhaps regretfully recognized too late. But even when the sense of choice is low, the pressure of different possibilities still exists—perhaps to retreat, as suggested by this harassed woman:

> I'm tired and don't like the place that we live and I am going back home. I want to be near my family and I want my mother now . . . I am never out. I haven't been out now for six years. I hardly ever get a chance to go anywhere. I really could go, but I am so tired at the end of the day I don't want to go anywhere.

[21] Alan L. Otten, "Politics and People," *Wall Street Journal,* September 20, 1973, p. 10.

Briefly summarized in her remarks are contending values about being a wife and mother versus being a daughter, being at home versus going out, working hard versus giving up. Her conflicts about her marriage (to a navy man) and her children (she has five) are leading to the purchase of moving services, changes in household style, and, with her mother to baby-sit, perhaps greater use of entertainment facilities.

Subjective conflict is seen as a natural accompaniment of some life circumstances:

> Sixteen is lots of activities, always on the go. You are in the prime of life. It is happy years. You don't have worries other people have, you don't have to worry where your dinner is coming from. It is sometimes hard to make decisions, what to wear, the right thing to wear when you are going someplace. And sometimes you have so many places to go you don't know where to go. It is hard to decide.

This girl sees her age as a time when some large decisions seem remote or minor compared to the nuances of clothing, and she feels no conflict over whether to go out at all but rather frets a bit over where to go.

The contention of values within individuals affects their marketing roles in all spheres. It is visible in their intimate marketing relationships, as shown in psychiatric and clinical psychological literature, where case studies are replete with examples of struggles with what one wishes to give and to get. Freud describes a characteristic example of a boy who reacted against the birth of a brother with great feelings of anger and frustration. Fearful of his own rage, he became very passive, behaving toward others in a kind and polite, but cold, manner. He longed to receive love but did not know how to go about it. He withdrew from talking, and in his daydreams he became a great orator who by making speeches could receive more admiration than others.[22] Other examples of the pervasiveness of subjective conflict in marketing become visible when people show concern about what they should offer in the labor market. This concern becomes bound up with what kind of preparation to buy—for instance, whether or not to continue acquiring schooling. Where to sell one's services (California, a big city, a small business) may loom larger as a source of brooding than whether to offer one's skills in marketing or in finance. In making decisions of these kinds, the individual's inner conflict is often between such values as hedonism versus service to others, being successful on a large scale versus the satisfactions of small-town life, maintaining personal dignity and self-control versus being expressive, solving novel problems versus meeting repetitive demands, and identifying with lower-class blue-collar work versus middle-class white-collar work. These polarities are simplifications of the issues that interact complex-

[22]Sigmund Freud, *The Problem of Anxiety* (New York: W. W. Norton & Company, Inc., 1936).

ly within people with varying degrees of force over time as the career line develops.

Within the commercial marketing system, buyers and sellers of traditional products and services undergo conflict about specific decisions at various levels of commitment or immediacy. When a customer is being wooed by several suppliers to buy their products or to contract for their ongoing services, he may have difficulty deciding what weight to give to the value of making such decisions "rational," perhaps with sealed bids and a decision rule to accept the lowest bidder, or to the value of relying on his friendship with one of the salesmen. One study of suppliers to a major manufacturer showed that there were some who felt uneasy about whether to insist on their technical expertise as the major value at issue or to yield to the purchasing agents' interest in friendly discussions at local bars.

Whether decisions are large or small, they are not exempt from the awareness that one's personal and social values are competing for expression. Dramatic examples occur when the conflict over choices to be made becomes so pronounced that personal integration is threatened—a phenomenon not infrequent, for example, among people redecorating or moving to a new home. More casual examples are gleaned from interviews in which consumers were asked about deciding to buy something.

> The most recent decision was with some chocolates at the store. I thought, will the family get more enjoyment from these chocolates than from candy bars? I bought them for purely selfish reasons—I crave them, but it was a difficult decision. It was a luxury item, but I splurged.

•   •   •

> I like the best quality of everything I buy. I feel that you get what you pay for. I'm not satisfied with less than the best. I've tried several times to buy less expensive toilet paper, but I always go back to a more expensive one.

In these two brief instances are glimpsed the fleeting manifestations of different ongoing values confronting each other: the value of pleasing the family versus the urge to gratify oneself, impulsiveness versus deliberation, economy versus luxury, high-quality standards versus petty savings, implicit sensory discriminations versus pragmatic self-concepts. The two women are interesting to compare, as the first is a lower-middle-class woman who feels guilty about having a bit of luxury, whereas the second is an upper-middle-class woman who feels that luxury is really her due.

It should be noted that subjective conflict is not solely or necessarily a negative or an unpleasant condition. The term *conflict* has negative connotations, and the common tendency is to assume that people want to avoid, diminish, or resolve it. Various behavioral theories depend upon the tenet that the individual seeks to be consistent within himself, to order his values, attitudes, emotions in an internally consistent manner, and to fit his behavior to them. The Festinger theory of cognitive dissonance thus predicts that the person who engages in a behavior that is not consistent with his concept of himself or his motives will perceive a discomfort or tension and seek to reduce it. [23]

Perhaps insufficient attention has been given to the variation in people's *tolerance of cognitive dissonance.* While it seems true that most people do not suffer ambiguity or ambivalence very well, it is also evident that cognitive dissonance can be actively sought or lived with. Consistency theories are single valued and lack the nuance to correspond to the subtlety of human affairs and motives. Some people seem to take delight in owning possessions that they criticize, in doing things they think are wrong, in failing to seek resolutions to dilemmas, or to persist in situations that make them anxious, and so forth. Large normative generalizations may not be helpful in the kinds of instances that seem contradictory, such as persisting in selling practices that lose money, running advertisements whose effects cannot practically be evaluated, or buying foods the family does not like. In struggling with one's aims in such situations, the generalization may help in insisting on a search for the consistency that *must* somehow be at work. Thus, if a self-actualizing theory is postulated, a suicide's constructive aim (call for help?) must be sought until it is discerned. Then again, contrary aims might be admitted, and however arrived at, a certain autonomy and validity granted to destructiveness, disorder, pleasure in pain, or even inconsistency *per se* as a motive. Such inconsistency seems implied by Moskowitz's report of a study showing that the ten brands whose television advertising women disliked the most included Right Guard deodorant, Crest toothpaste, and Bold detergent. [24] Bold's rise in the market was very strong nevertheless, and both Right Guard and Crest were leaders in their fields.

It might be reasoned that the ultimate criterion of dissonance is in the person, that the term is always relative, and that it is possibly being misapplied. More probably, as there are always numerous contending values in the personality, some behaviors must inevitably be dissonant and, equally inevitably, must be tolerated. Different circumstances are simultaneously addressed to different levels in one's hierarchy of values. Pleasure can be found in such conflicts when they are taken as sources of personal complexity, excitement, mystery, variety, and change. The more marketing spheres in which a person moves, the more different values are likely to be called upon, the more different roles he plays. This can mean greater conflicts among values, but also greater satisfaction or ingenuity in techniques for resolving the conflicts.

Outside of private marketing research studies such as in the work of Social Research, Inc., the specific structure and content of the individual's subjectivity in determining his marketing actions has not been much explored.

---

[23]Leon A. Festinger, *A Theory of Cognitive Dissonance* (Stanford: Stanford University Press, 1957).

[24]M. Moskowitz, "The Money Tree," *Chicago Sun-Times,* May 24, 1970, p. 77.

Some suggestions in this direction are presented in the Boyd and Levy discussion of consumption systems, [25] in the collection of consumer behavior cases by W. T. Tucker, [26] and in the model being developed by Daniel B. Williams. [27]

Transactional Conflict

Transactional conflict refers to *the encounter of the differences inherent in the goals of buyers and sellers.* Reavis Cox calls the things that sellers do forces that they can use to mold the responses of buyers to serve their interests. In one of the few instances in traditional marketing literature to face the fact, Cox is explicit about the resultant conflict:

> To the buyer and more particularly to the industrial buyer or the self-conscious and organized consumer buyer, they are forces to be resisted and re-directed. Conflicts between seller and buyer arise from the fact that what benefits the seller most does not necessarily serve the buyer best.
>
> This divergence of interest between seller and buyer is one source for the belief sometimes expressed that marketing (and more specifically selling) is a form of combat. [28]

People come to the marketplace with their multitudinous goals and aims. Because so much attention is ordinarily given to the aims and procedures of sellers, in marketing text books, the nature of the conflict may be interestingly examined by taking the vantage point of the buyer. To begin with, the theoretically initial unit in marketing is the buyer. As an apparently insatiable "wanting" organism, the buyer experiences the world and wants it. This phenomenon is readily observable in children and often visible in adults. With little socialization, the impulse is to take something merely because it is there. The paradigm is the infant, reaching for anything available and trying to incorporate it. But various conditions arise to inform the novice and two are of basic importance: *One can't have everything,* and *one must give something in return.* The first is the condition for making choices, and the second creates exchanges. These conditions require assessments of worth and of resources, of motives, value discriminations, and economics. If one must choose among alternatives and if one must give something in return, it is necessary to decide how important the object is, how much it is worth pursuing, and how much one is willing to give for it.

[25]Harper W. Boyd and Sidney J. Levy, "New Dimension in Consumer Analysis," *Harvard Business Review,* November-December 1963, pp. 129—40.

[26]W. T. Tucker, *Foundations for a Theory of Consumer Behavior* (New York: Holt, Rinehart & Winston, Inc., 1967).

[27]Daniel B. Williams (doctoral dissertation, Northwestern University).

[28]Reavis Cox, "Three-in-One Marketing," in *Modern Marketing Strategy,* ed. Edward C. Bursk and John F. Chapman (Boston: Harvard University Press, 1964), p. 73.

The urgency of the buyer, his force of desire and willingness to fight are often modest. In the everyday situation, purchasing common objects hardly seems to involve conflict, yet in both subtle and gross ways various kinds of self-assertion and ingenuity are needed to reach one's buyer goals. It may be useful to observe this in terms of generic requirements, circumstances requiring unusual initiative from the buyer, and the situation of the monopsonist.

GENERIC QUALIFICATION

In many situations of the mass-market variety, only some minimum generic qualifications are necessary to be a customer at all. It is routinely recognized that time, place, and cost specifications must be fulfilled. The customer knows he can be a buyer if he appears at the time of the sale with enough money; almost anyone who shows up at the checkout counter with a loaf of bread, and the fifty-two cents it costs, can have it. The accommodation of the customer to the situation is relatively minimal: there are likely to be many loaves available, waiting time is short, and there is wide latitude as to who the buyer can be.

There do remain broad constraints. The customer has to behave with some semblance of sanity. If abusive or naked, he may be arrested instead of sold bread; if a young child, he may be pushed aside or overlooked by aggressive adults. He may want to charge the purchase or to buy more loaves than the sale permits each buyer, thus distinguishing himself from the routine buyer. Nevertheless, the customer in such situations is likely to perceive that no special demands are made of him, that he is not being discriminated against, that the conditions for being a buyer are, by and large, generic ones. He may compete for favor (e.g., not having his bread squashed by poor packing) by being congenial with the checkout girl, but he usually does not have to compete with other customers, and there would not be much point to offering to pay more for the loaf of bread.

In situations of generic qualification, the buyer is apt to be relatively unselfconscious. He expresses his usual motivations as these relate to food choices, supermarket behavior, and so forth, but he is not prone to examine his qualifications to be a buyer, nor to devise special strategies to cope with the seller.

THE DETERMINED BUYER

In contrast to the situations of generic qualification where the buyer limits are very broad, on many occasions it is necessary to practice being a "determined" or attractive buyer in the sense of being one who gets to be a buyer in the face of special obstacles. The basic issue is actual or potential denial of supply, but the participants, the sellers' reasons, the locales, and the means of combat have a particular character.

1. Sharply Focused Market Segmentation. The definition of who is acceptable to the seller is a precise or narrow one and therefore tends to exclude all others.

- Women are ordinarily expected to be purchasers of brassieres. A man may buy one but has to overcome social and psychological obstacles to do so. To be an attractive buyer, then, he will need to make special efforts, unlike the bread buyer, to screw up his courage, to explain his intention to the seller, perhaps to throw himself on her mercy in an ingratiating way.
- Minors are not supposed to be able to buy cigarettes, liquor, or tickets to adult movies. Being an attractive buyer means getting others to wink at the law, finding sellers who are indifferent or who enjoy corrupting young people, or finding other adults who will act as surrogate purchasers.

2. Limited Supply. Whenever there is not enough for the good to go around, the potential buyer has to compete with others for the scarce resource. In doing this, he confronts the strategy being used by the seller and decides whether to be obedient to it or attempt to circumvent it.

- The widespread use of first come, first served, means that customers are faced with deadlines for getting in orders or that patrons must queue up so that earlier ones get the benefit of their seniority before the supply is gone. The potential buyer who fears he will be left out may devise methods to improve his position. Sending a messenger ahead is one method. Having someone "save my place" is a common technique, one that arouses particular resentment among those who see the empty but unavailable place—and sometimes refuse to honor it. Not infrequently, the queue is aggressively destroyed to produce a more favorable reallocation of positions.

A grander example is provided by the powerful situation of the Organization of Petroleum Exporting Countries (OPEC). M. A. Adelman comments that "the genie is out of the bottle. The OPEC nations have had a great success with the threat of embargo and will not put the weapon away." He is not sanguine about his prescription, believing that it is late for the resistance that would have been effective earlier.

> The consuming countries can have cheapness and security only by a clean break with the past: get the multinational oil companies out of crude oil marketing; let them remain as producers under contract and as buyers of crude to transport, refine and sell as products. The real owners, the producing nations must then assume the role of sellers and they should be assisted in competing the price of crude oil down. But this would only minimize conflict and confrontation; it is too late to avoid them. [29]

3. Preferential Treatment. Limited supply means a limitation on the number of successful buyers and often becomes a basis for preferential treatment. In addition, limited supply may be created by a limiting of access to the product or service: there is enough, but the individual is being excluded. Buyers have various techniques for gaining preferential treatment.

[29]M. A. Adelman, "How Real Is the World Oil Shortage?" *Wall Street Journal,* February 9, 1973, p. 12.

- *Transformation.* Conditions are created by sellers that require the successful buyer to be a kind of person, to behave in prescribed ways. One must wear a tie, read a French menu, appreciate classical music, know someone in the trade, be prosperous, be married, etc. The motivated buyer may transform himself by actually getting married, studying French, or earning enough money to afford access to the place, service, or product. He may bluff a transformation by pretending he knows someone "on the inside," fake an address, use a nonethnic name, disguise himself, steal a credit card, etc. In the acquisition of products, stealing is a method that provides preferential access. It may seem to pervert the word buyer, but paying nothing, getting something FREE is a consumer goal sellers recognize when *they* set it as a condition.

- *Membership.* Belonging to a group devoted to some common purpose is a widespread formal way of gaining preferential treatment. By their patterns of belonging, buyers develop access to a great variety of products and services. The "joiner" attitude in America has shifted away somewhat from the traditional fraternal organizations, but memberships in clubs, plans, and associations may make it easier, perhaps cheaper, more or less privileged, to obtain books, travel, insurance, cultural experiences, liquor in a dry community, time on a golf course. Many memberships are so casually obtained as to imply generic qualification, but others set up obstacles for the determined buyer—unusual fees, achievements, complex application forms, sponsorship.

- *Money.* Preferential status may be purchased, as with many memberships. In other instances, the purchase takes the form of bribery, tipping, and paying premiums, as ways of buying freedom from traffic tickets, getting better tables, seats, hotel rooms, improved position on a waiting list for parking privileges, etc. As with stealing, these are *sub rosa* buying activities; but paying a premium, buying something one does not want (e.g., furniture or old carpets to get a house or apartment) are ways a buyer makes himself more attractive to a seller.

- *Persuasion.* Noneconomic strategies are also helpful and necessary in situations of nongeneric qualification. Being beguiling or friendly, stressing one's urgent need, flattering the clerk, demanding attention, complaining to the manager—an infinite array of interpersonal emotional payments are required in buying situations. An effective buyer calls on a repertoire of such behavior (whether deliberate or spontaneous) to get housecalls from craftsmen, servicemen, physicians, help from haughty or indifferent clerks, early delivery from industrial sellers, or a positive answer in a courtship.

- *Law.* Using legal means is a forceful method of persuasion. Ordinarily, the law is called on when people feel that they are generically qualified to be buyers but are nevertheless being denied supply, deprived of their access to goods that should be available to all—medical treatment, housing, education, etc. In addition, the law's support is sought when preferential buyer status is desired—country club, special school, etc.—but is being withheld for reasons regarded as tangential, such as bias toward race, religion, ethnicity, sex, or age. To the extent that improved products and pricing contribute to the buyer's having preferential treatment, or improved position relative to the seller, any legal suits against sellers may serve this function.

- *Trouble.* Buyers make trouble for sellers who displease them by complaining, demanding services, badmouthing, making a scene, vandalism, etc. It has been noted that in desperate response, landlords are giving up the struggle. The National Association of Home Builders says that tenant-landlord conflicts are apparently making apartments less attractive as investments for building owners, adding to the trend to convert apartments to condominiums.

MONOPSONISTS

Monopsonists are a form of determined buyer that merits note; they might be called warden buyers, as they are customers who buy from relatively captive sellers. These situations come about when buyers tend to have unusual power because the number of alternatives among buyers are few, or because the seller has entered into a special relationship with the buyer. Prominent examples of warden buyers are large corporations such as General Motors and Sears, who are in a position to dominate a supplier who sells them his total output, or buyers of military equipment, of rare gems (Richard Burton), and of great art. Some interesting features that may appear in the behavior of warden buyers include the following:

- *Advertising.* To make themselves attractive, warden buyers (and nonmonopsonists, but other special kinds of buyers) reverse the usual procedure and make special efforts to inform sellers that they are in the market. Some businesses routinely announce that they buy and sell (books, cars, furniture); publishers' agents announce that they will be in town to buy manuscripts. Small buyers shop with announcements on local bulletin boards, and large buyers will make known through trade channels that they wish to buy certain major equipment and may solicit bids from sellers.
- *Product evaluation.* Powerful warden buyers can take unusual measures to exercise judgment about products. Some organizations set up stringent requirements for seller demonstrations and tight specifications. Others have laboratory facilities to analyze and test products, or they run "test markets" by permitting employees to try out proposed supplies before committing to a major purchase.
- *Market research.* Large warden buyers may study their suppliers in a manner analogous to the way sellers study consumers. A major corporation studied several small suppliers and learned much about the problems these sellers faced in submitting bids and dealing with the company's purchasing agents and engineers. The company became a more attractive buyer by applying the marketing concept in the direction of trying to understand and meet the needs of sellers.

Transactional conflict radiates into the special relationship to the market of each market segment. An example of particular contemporary interest is the ghetto consumer.

THE GHETTO CONSUMER

Marketing is often criticized for its inability to meet the needs of those at the lowest end of the socioeconomic scale. The low-income or ghetto consumer, according to the critics, does not participate in equitable exchanges but must contend with various illegal and discriminatory practices. In effect, the ghetto consumer is portrayed as both a combatant and a victim of marketing agents and their activities. The following paragraphs examine the manifestations of conflict between ghetto consumers and marketers and the attempts to account for the causes and conditions of such conflicts.

Three broad charges are directed at marketers:

1. Marketing practices in the ghetto are exploitative and discriminatory. That is, relative to the more affluent nonghetto consumer, the ghetto consumer pays higher prices, often for inferior products, and at excessive credit rates.
2. Marketers in the ghetto employ illegal tactics. Such techniques as deceptive advertising or bait-and-switch practices are said to be rampant in the ghetto.
3. The present buyer-seller relationships are thought to perpetuate asymmetrical distributions of rewards, opportunities, and power at the expense of the ghetto resident.

The research evidence to date relating to the above issues is mixed. Yet, the literature is rich with numerous instances of conflict.

Pricing practices have been attacked as particularly exploitative. In general, pricing abuses may be classified in regard to the level, representation, and flexibility of application.

A number of studies have investigated the charge that prices are higher in the ghetto. As can be seen in Table 4-1, the evidence indicates that in some instances prices are higher, while in others they are not.[30] Price comparisons are difficult to make, since much of consumption centers around such non-price factors as psychological needs, services, and packaging. Clearly, simple price comparisons are not sufficient and may even be misleading. What are needed are investigations comparing the entire complex of product service offerings in light of situational conditions.

Prices can be misrepresented in a number of ways. Caplovitz cites the following incident as a "typical episode" of exploitative buyer-seller relations in the ghetto. The speaker is a black housewife in New York:

> I heard an ad on the radio about a special bargain on washing machines for only $100. After I ordered it and had it installed, I got a bill for $200. I said I wouldn't pay it and they took it away. I paid a $50 down-payment, and they never gave it back to me. I'm just glad I did not have to pay the balance.[31]

How can such a discrepancy exist between an initially agreed-upon price and the final bill? In essence, the merchant includes "additional charges" in his final bill. Or, if the law requires the seller to list both the price and the finance charges on a bill or a contract (as is the case in New York), the seller may conveniently delay sending the consumer his copy of the sale until the goods have been delivered and a down payment has been made. The contract

[30]See Reed Moyer, *Macro Marketing: A Social Perspective* (New York: John Wiley & Sons, Inc., 1972), pp. 126-34, for a summary of some of the studies indicated in Table 4-1.

[31]David Caplovitz, *The Poor Pay More* (New York: The Free Press, 1967), p. 147.

TABLE 4-1
Comparison of Research Investigating and Level of
Prices in Ghetto and Low-Income Areas

Study	Product	Finding
U.S. Bureau of Labor investigation of chain, large independents, and small independent food stores (1966) [1]	Food	". . . no significant differences in prices charged by food stores located in low-income areas versus those charged by stores in higher income areas, when the same type of stores . . . , the same qualities of foods, and the same sizes of packages are compared."
Hearings before Special Studies Committee of Committee on Government Operations, House of Representatives (1967) [2]	Food	Food prices were from 6 to 15 percent higher in ghetto stores versus stores in higher-income areas. On welfare paydays, prices were 9.5 percent higher in ghetto stores and 2.5 percent higher in nonghetto stores compared with the period two days before paydays.
Consumer Action Program investigation in Brooklyn, New York (1967) [3]	Food	Food prices were from 3.5 to 6 percent higher in the ghetto versus nonghetto stores.
New York Council on Consumer Affairs investigation (1967) [4]	Food	Prices on welfare paydays were "about 15 percent" higher than several days before payday.
Marcus investigation in the Watts and Culver City areas of Greater Los Angeles (1969) [5]	Food	For all foods, ghetto store prices were .7 percent lower than nonghetto store prices. For all foods except meat and produce, ghetto store prices were 4 percent higher than nonghetto store prices.
Federal Trade Commission investigation of prices in the District of Columbia (1966) [6]	Furniture and Appliances	"On the average, goods purchased for $100 at wholesale sold for $255 in the low income market stores, compared with $159 in general market stores." Low-income store prices for appliances were as much as 80 percent higher than the general market store prices.

[1] U.S. Bureau of Labor Statistics, "A Study of Prices Charged in Food Stores Located in Low and Higher Income Areas of Six Large Cities," February 1966. Reprinted in *National Commission on Food Marketing*, Technical Study No. 10 (June 1966), pp. 122—44.

[2] U.S. Congress, House, Hearing before Special Studies Committee of Committee on Government Operations, *Consumer Problems of the Poor*, 90th Cong., 2nd sess., October 12, November 24—25, 1967, pp. 7—40.

[3] Reed Moyer, *Macro Marketing: A Social Perspective* (New York: John Wiley & Sons, Inc., 1972), p. 130.

[4] U.S. Congress, *Consumer Problems of the Poor*, p. 20.

[5] Burton H. Marcus, "Similarity of Ghetto and Nonghetto Food Costs," *Journal of Marketing Research*, August 1969, pp. 365—68.

[6] *Economic Report on Installment Credit and Retail Sales Practices of District of Columbia Retailers* (Washington, D.C.: Federal Trade Commission, 1968). Reprinted in Frederick D. Sturdivant, ed., *The Ghetto Market Place* (New York: The Free Press, 1969), pp. 76—107.

may then contain the new inflated price. As one may surmise, however, the evidence of price misrepresentation is often largely anecdotal and difficult to prove. [32]

Still another charge directed at ghetto marketers is their use of such illegal tactics as the bait-and-switch ploy, which is often described in the literature. Using this technique, the merchant offers a product at a low price (the "bait"); after the customer is enticed into the store, pressure is applied to induce the sale of a more-expensive item (the "switch"). Sometimes the seller will stress the advantages of the more-expensive item and disparage the qualities of the lower-priced item, while in other instances he may claim that the lower-priced item is unavailable or must be ordered from the manufacturer. In many cases, however, it is difficult to ascertain the difference between normal modes of persuasion and the bait-and-switch technique. Just where the line should be drawn between accepted and excessive persuasion tactics is difficult to define.

Another illegal tactic is product substitution, that is, replacing the new product sold with a similar-but-used or defective product. Caplovitz quotes the following experience of a Puerto Rican woman in New York as an example of this practice:

> I bought a TV set from a First Avenue store. It was a used set which was sold as new. After seven days it broke down. The store took it back and returned it in two weeks. It broke down again and they took it for thirty days. They brought it back and it broke down one week later. They took it away and I asked for a refund because there was a guarantee of ninety days which had not run out. But they wouldn't give me back my $100 or bring me another TV.[33]

Since the ghetto consumer earns a relatively low income, such practices as the above are especially injurious.

The final criticism of marketing in the ghetto is that exchanges often involve asymmetric relationships. The merchant, for example, is usually in a strong position and can use credit and other means to gain from the consumer:

> The proverbial "dollar down, dollar a week" accurately describes credit terms on ghetto retail transactions. Payments are low to reduce their burden. They are made often to keep close tabs on the customer and to get him into the store. Most customers visit the store to pay on their accounts. This arrangement gives the merchant repeated opportunities to make additional sales. This tying of the customer to a store is a familiar arrangement to many ghetto residents who have emigrated from the South. There, as sharecroppers, they had similar linkages with the company store. [34]

---

[32]An exception is the Sturdivant and Wilhelm study which, for example, found that the credit prices to three different racial-ethnic couples varied from $418 to $507 for the same television set in a store in the Watts neighborhood of Los Angeles.

[33]Caplovitz, *op. cit.*, p. 150.

[34]Moyer, *op. cit.*, p. 136.

Moreover, the seller often has the advantage of possessing more information and knowledge with respect to products, transactions, and financial and legal matters. Even though the courts are theoretically designed to serve the interests of all, the merchant is usually more aware of legal procedures and opportunities and as a result makes "extensive use of the courts in collecting debts." [35]

The above paragraphs illustrate instances of conflict as viewed primarily from the perspective of the consumer. But these manifestations of conflict do not reveal all the forces and determinants shaping the marketer-consumer relationships in the ghetto. The ghetto merchant is also confronted with many diverse patterns of conflict which both directly and indirectly affect buyer-seller interactions. To gain insight into the processes of conflict within the ghetto, one must examine the pressures and constraints typical of the environment of the ghetto businessman.

For the businessman, the market in the ghetto can be characterized as one of relatively low volume and high costs, a condition hardly conducive to low prices. Furthermore, store rental and insurance rates are often higher in the ghetto than in the nonghetto environment, and vandalism, pilferage, and shoplifting may be rampant. Thus the merchant is frequently caught between the demands of low-income consumers for low prices and the adverse economic realities of his situation. Attitudes toward the sellers are complicated, sometimes by such binds as poor support for entrepreneurs who are members of one's own ethnic group coupled with antagonism toward nonmembers who are exploiters by local definition. Even if their prices are fair, the latter are taking money out of the community. The nonghetto merchant contends with pressures of lesser magnitude in situations where demand allows for greater economies of scale and subsequent savings for the consumer.

Even though higher prices may be justified by higher costs, some people will interpret the higher costs as merely additional evidence of the disadvantage of the ghetto dweller. Ardent defenders of the right of ghetto dwellers to share in the goods produced by the society have gone so far as to suggest that the looters who took television sets from stores during the riots following Martin Luther King's assassination were not so much stealing as expressing a new definition of property.

Some of the issues raised by considering certain populations to be exploited have to do with the minimum standard of living thought to be a citizen's basic right. Prices become less relevant when one's values dictate that everyone should have a telephone because its absence implies an untenable isolation or that doctor's fees should deprive no one of medical care. In other instances, the values concern the level of access that should be available to

[35] *Economic Report on Installment Credit and Retail Sales Practices of District of Columbia Retailers* (Washington, D.C.: Federal Trade Commission, 1968), p. xiii.

people to participate in the marketing system: ghetto dwellers are spoken of as being trapped in their neighborhoods or uninformed about their rights or privileges. Another point of view considers ghetto dwellers as being like children in their relative weakness (Steuart Henderson Britt has termed them "the vulnerables"), requiring protection from their inability to evaluate marketing approaches or to withstand attractive promotion.

Transactional conflicts are inevitable because as each participant pursues his own interest, he comes up against the diverse interests of others. Even though a harmonious transaction may be to the ultimate benefit of both, the calculus of mutual benefit is often hard to determine and may not be visible to, or sought by, the participants. Some designers and R & D people are seen as being more interested in their designs and researches than in the marketability of their results—in the eyes of the commercial marketer; that is, because the corporation pays them salaries, they are able to resist the power of the marketing manager. Another interesting example in the distribution system is provided by the manufacturer's representative. As a salesman, a man in the middle, he has to struggle with both his sources of supply and his customers. He may present himself as a powerless person in this struggle.

> The Rep is never really in control of his own fate. All he can control is how hard he works. His job is, of course, to induce; but he can't compel his wholesalers to buy his lines. He can't make his factories keep him competitive or perform on their promises. And he doesn't have much maneuverability.36

One of the problems faced by such commissioned salesmen is that of arbitrary termination. The National Council of Salesman's Organizations seeks a law protecting the salesman against being terminated without just cause, citing a Puerto Rican law which shows "respect for the salesman and for his right to just treatment."

Even a brief overview of transactional issues would be incomplete without a reminder of the brilliant work of Erving Goffman in analyzing the complex interplay of face-to-face relations in everyday life. 37

36Charles Horton, "The M/R and His Role in Our Industry: An Interview with Marvin Leffler," *Supply House Times,* September 1973, p. 65.

37Erving Goffman, *Relations in Public: Microstudies of the Public Order* (New York: Basic Books, Inc., Publishers, 1971).

CHAPTER FIVE

Commercial and Social Marketing Conflict

COMMERCIAL MARKETING CONFLICT

The general meaning of the form of conflict called *competition* is any *striving for comparative distiction*. The purpose of striving is to win out in conflict with oneself or with another by surpassing some alternative performance with reference to whatever goal is at issue. Competition in the commercial arena is a most familiar phenomenon. Customers recognize that sellers compete for their favor and that this is possible when there are choices available in the marketplace. The most notable and obvious means of competition is price. In one sense, prices are competitive when they are the same for the same product; in another sense, a competitive price is a lower one. Since sellers seek to find some differential advantage in appealing to customers, any other means may be used, in addition to price or instead of price.

The issues raised by competition are numerous, and there is a large literature on the subject. These issues relate to the role of competition in the social system, to questions of efficiency, degrees of concentration, barriers to entry, and an array of legislation. An excellent summary discussion by Louis W. Stern and John R. Grabner, Jr., is presented in *Managerial Analysis in Marketing* by Frederick Sturdivant and others,[1] and it is not necessary to go over similar ground here. The present purpose is to highlight the role of conflict in competition, as the customary formal discussions seem to "lose the name of action," so that competition often sounds as mild as cooperation.

The actualities of competition are most noticeable when specific examples are described, cases that demonstrate how competition goes on, the intensity of the participants, and their various battlegrounds.

The delight in competition that is considered peculiarly American is exemplified in the outlook of the Adolph Coors Company. According to William K. Coors, the company's chairman and president, "If you can't

---

[1] Frederick D. Sturdivant *et al.*, *Managerial Analysis in Marketing* (Glenview, Ill.: Scott, Foresman & Company, 1970).

fight competition, you don't need to survive." It is a pure and fundamental Darwinian statement, accepting the challenge and the consequences. The *Wall Street Journal* comments that no single trait so dominates this feisty company as its obvious pleasure in coming to grips with its competition, and that despite many obstacles it has grown to be the nation's fourth largest brewer. Coors further asserts, "I take a lot of satisfaction in opposing all the forces that would like to put us out of business." He sees these forces as the three giants of the brewing industry, who together hold 45 percent of the national market; numerous labor unions; civil-rights groups; antialcohol individuals, or "drys," who remain a potent force in much of the company's marketing area; and the Federal Trade Commission, which has ordered Coors to stop fixing prices and to alter certain practices relating to its distribution.

Ralph Cassady contributes an instance of commercial conflict at the retail level. Offered as an example of the "price skirmish," it illustrates how competitors can flare up with antagonism, even to their mutual disadvantage:

> One of the most interesting price skirmishes which has come to the attention of this writer, however, was one that broke out in upper Manhattan, New York, between two grocery vendors several years ago, involving oddly enough, the use of green groceries as a competitive weapon. Price conflicts rarely revolve around unbranded merchandise since price reductions of such items generally go unchallenged because of the possibility of wide quality variation.

> The encounter involving price cutting of fruits and vegetables was precipitated when a merchant who had previously confined his efforts to the sale of green groceries decided to add canned goods. The move was deeply resented by the manager of a small neighborhood supermarket, who evidently considered this an invasion of his territory and thus a threat to his business success. He, therefore, informed his competitor that he intended to resist the move, by drastic means if necessary.

> There being no sign of capitulation by early the following afternoon, the first move was made by the supermarket manager who started to undercut the invader on the prices of fruits and vegetables. The initial reductions brought prices approximately to cost or less-than-cost levels. For example, strawberries normally selling at 25 cents a box were reduced to 19 cents, which quotation the invader immediately undercut with a price of 15 cents. When this price was met by the opponent, the invader began giving strawberries away free of charge on a first-come, first-served basis, one pint of strawberries to a customer. Much the same thing happened with tomatoes, grapefruit, and cucumbers.

> The price cuts in the foregoing price skirmish were not publicized except, of course, by word of mouth. Nevertheless, it is interesting how quickly news spreads to the consumer in instances such as this. Within minutes consumer-buyers were gathering with two and three shopping bags in order to purchase what was being sold cheaply and to take advantage of the free offerings. Each vendor was attempting to attract customers to his own outlet or, rather, to keep customers from his opponent's establishment. In their attempt to hurt the "enemy," rational action momentarily gave way to emotional behavior, although neither adversary physically attacked the other.

This battle, which broke out at 1:30 P.M. was over by 3:30 P.M. when losses approximated $100 each, at which point reason undoubtedly overcame emotion. Thus, this skirmish ended almost as quickly as it started, apparently because of its costliness in relation to the limited resources of the opposing vendors. The speed of termination undoubtedly was a major factor in confining the conflict to these two establishments and preventing its spread to other neighborhood food stores.

The result of the skirmish developing out of the introduction of canned goods by a greengrocer was that the invader was repelled in his attempt to add the new line. It is interesting that this might have been only a preliminary encounter to a long drawn out action by the invader to gain a beachhead had it not been for the fact that the invader's landlord pointed out to him that the terms of his lease confined his retailing activity to the sale of fresh fruits and vegetables. [2]

Such competitive vehemence is certainly not restricted to neighborhood food stores. Allvine and Patterson discuss the competitive situation summed up in Figure 5-1, analyzing in detail how competition in the oil industry has affected the independent dealer through a variety of aggressive practices. [3] They note a pattern of several techniques used by major oil companies to "soften up" the price marketer, frequently followed by the *coup de grâce* of buying him out.

The foregoing rhetoric of the situation is not the way spokesmen for the major oil companies describe their actions. The independents say that the issue is not the keenness of competition, but the inordinate power of the majors; the latter are concerned with their own success and their demonstrated superiority, especially in the face of being so widely misunderstood and maligned when the Arab oil embargo first roiled the world's oil situation. The values involved move readily from technical questions to issues of fairness, the toleration to be afforded bigness and oligopoly, and the sympathy one feels for the underdog, the little guy. In this struggle, the independent companies plead their special nature and need for special treatment. They complain that the majors drive them out of business. Even larger companies can find the conflict so intense that such imagery as "competitive cannibalism" is used:

> Too often, however, these wars have degenerated into nothing more than competitive cannibalism, with gasoline being sold below cost and indeed, in some cases, even below the cost of crude oil at the wellhead. The pursuit of this

---

[2]Ralph Cassady, Jr., "The Price Skirmish—A Distinctive Pattern of Competitive Behavior," *California Management Review,* 7, No. 2 (Winter 1964), 11-16.

[3]Fred C. Allvine and James M. Patterson, *Competition, Ltd.: The Marketing of Gasoline* (Bloomington: Indiana University Press, 1972). See also, Fred C. Allvine and James M. Patterson, *Highway Robbery: An Analysis of the Gasoline Crisis* (Bloomington: Indiana University Press, 1974).

FIGURE 5-1

Recent Commentary on Competition
in the Oil Industry

kind of business practice is damaging to the entire oil industry. It forces independent service station dealers and distributors, most of whom are small in size
and weak in competitive power, out of business, and eventually results in the
growth of monopoly and in irreparable harm to the consumer . . . the type of
inequity that Government has a responsibility to prevent.[4]

The speaker is the president of Tidewater Oil Company, whose West
Coast operation had suffered from a Shell Oil one-cent differential pricing
approach. Shell's tactic was described as a natural reaction by the majors to
loss of share of market due to the improvement of the price marketers'
service stations.

They're knocking our socks off in too many areas. We can't sit still any
longer.

• • •

[4]*Ibid.*, pp. 137-38.

> These stations [price marketers] are modern, attractive and in fine locations. The operators advertise . . . the high quality of their products. In fact, they may be better attuned to the times than many long-established marketers and are setting interesting trends in large volume outlets . . .

> • • •

> In many cases the independent refiner and the cutrate marketers are operating from better facilities and better locations than the so-called major dealer, yet, generally speaking, they still expect to have a price advantage of 2 cents a gallon or more simply because they have not been classified as major company dealers. [5]

The implication of these remarks is that the major oil companies share the social value of permitting small and weak competitors to exist but do not think that it is fair for independents to receive the indulgence given small, weak units when they are in fact becoming large and powerful.

The weapons of competitive combat at times go beyond the conventional wars and skirmishes of pricing, enhancement of product quality, promotional creativity and vigor. Hugh Lacy, vice-president of the Urich Oil Company, indicates some of the measures taken when his company innovated with serve-yourself gasoline stations:

> The furor was unbelievable. Meetings of service station operators opposing us were held everywhere . . . City Councils were deluged with requests for anti-serve-yourself laws. Eleven states and hundreds of towns outlawed our operation . . . I received over forty death threats, and George R. "Frank" Urich received an equal number. In those days, he drove a truck and was fired upon on several occasions. I was run off the road by six men in a car who took off when I produced a 38 automatic. Our station help was beat up, creosol bottles were thrown against our buildings, and our neon signs were smashed with chains. [6]

Strife of this kind may seem unremarkable with its classical aura of familiar threat and physical violence among working-class personnel, trucks, and so forth. Less noticeable are the many examples of illegal activities in which personnel of higher status engage to move sharply or viciously against their competitors. Industrial espionage is widely practiced; steps are taken to distort the results of test marketing being conducted by other companies; and rumors are started to malign competitors' practices or the quality of their products. Such dirty tricks can escalate into "middle-class" sabotage as well, as Watergate illustrates in the political marketing arena. A former branch manager of the SCM Corporation testified that he had attended

[5]*Ibid.*, p. 116.
[6]*Ibid.*, p. 291.

regional sales meetings in which managers planned that their salesmen would tamper with competitors' office copier machines.[7] Sabotage in that industry included such events as jamming paper rollers, dropping objects in the toner tray, messing up the wiring, and puncturing ink tanks. Among the values being expressed in this competitive behavior was the basic one voiced by an ex-salesman of SCM, "In this business the end justifies the means."

Among the many realms and levels of marketing, the combat of the media has a long history ranging from newspaper wars to build circulation to brochures politely listing statistics describing the readers or viewers that a magazine or broadcast channel will deliver to a prospective advertiser. Even in the higher reaches of esoteric intellectual debate where the battle is joined on a melange of issues—literary criticism, political theory, and social comment— the journals fight it out with verbal violence. The differing positions of *Commentary* and the *New York Review of Books* are expounded by Philip Nobile,[8] Dennis Wrong,[9] and others, leading to polarized positions by those who pay attention. Nobile concluded that "the *Review* is still champ, still the biggest game in town," while John Chamberlain, who reviewed his book in the *Wall Street Journal,* asserts, "For myself, I'll still take *Commentary.*"

Thus, competitive conflict ranges from physical attack to eloquence. Within the conventional marketing system, each enterprise puts forth its aims and determines its means. Outside the conventional marketing system are similar forms of conflict, but the means are more blatantly illegal.

ILLEGAL MARKETING: THE SHADOW SYSTEM

An important—yet generally neglected—area of study in marketing is the role played by illegal marketing practices, collectively referred to here as the *shadow system.* Ranging from hijacking and theft on the one hand to fencing and resale on the other, illegal marketing practices amounted to more than $16 billion in losses to businesses in 1973 alone.[10]

Typically, retailers and other businesses must contend with three broad classes of adversaries who employ illegal tactics. The first class consists of crimes committed by the common criminal and includes burglary, robbery, hijacking, and similar crimes of theft. The goods stolen by these methods are often resold to the public either directly (through personal contact on street

[7] John Emshwiller, "If Your Copy Machine Doesn't Work, Maybe It Has Been Sabotaged," *Wall Street Journal,* September 11, 1973, p. 1.

[8] Philip Nobile, *Intellectual Skywriting: Literary Politics and the New York Review of Books* (Washington, D.C.: Charterhouse, 1974).

[9] Dennis Wrong, "The Case of the New York Review," *Commentary,* 50, No. 5 (November 1970), pp. 49-63.

[10] U.S. Congress, Senate Hearings before the Select Committee on Small Business, *Criminal Redistribution (Fencing) Systems,* 93rd Cong., 1st sess., Part 1, p. 1.

corners, in taverns, or even in the home) or indirectly (through professional middlemen, or "fences," who deal in illegal merchandise and supply retailers). Consider the following example which illustrates the relationships between the thief and the fence and between the fence and the buyer:

> . . . a thief locates a warehouse filled with TV sets. He notes the quantity and quality of the merchandise and informs his fence. The fence offers the thief a price for about one hundred sets and names a drop or delivery location. The drop may be another warehouse, a garage, or loft or store. The fence makes sure the drop is set to receive the goods. When delivery is made, the fence checks the goods and pays the thief. He then removes identification marks from the goods and the containers, or he may repackage the goods. The fence removes the goods in a truck to his place of business which has the appearance of a legitimate establishment. The fence informs retail merchants, jobbers or other buyers that he has exceptional buys on TV sets, well below the market price.[11]

Of course, not all fences operate legitimate businesses. Some are laborers or blue-collar or white-collar workers who supplement their incomes illegally. Some are drug pushers who have been forced to accept goods instead of cash for their wares. Finally, others are more professional go-betweens, sometimes acting as brokers who never see the goods with which they deal.

Organized crime and the professional criminal comprise the second class of malefactors that business must face. Though representing the most successful and managerially oriented category of the shadow system, organized crime is one of the most elusive and unknown. As an illustration of the "marketing" activities performed by the underworld, the following example depicts a typical "hijacking" operation where a truckload of goods is stolen and ultimately sold to consumers. Such thefts are estimated to total $1.5 billion per year.[12] The example was gleaned from testimony of a convicted safecracker-hijacker before the United States Senate.[13]

The classic theft begins with the existence of a valuable cargo—a load of liquor, meats, clothes, or pharmaceuticals often worth more than $100,000 at retail. The key man in the hijacking is the trucking company dispatcher or other knowledgeable employee (Figure 5-2 shows the distribution channels). The dispatcher knows the value of the cargo shipments as well as the time, place, and route of delivery. Typically, the dishonest dispatcher will meet with a contact man in the local tavern or restaurant and inform him of the cargo. The contact man (who may or may not work directly for the underworld) will relay the information to his connections in organized crime. If these individuals deem the opportunity suitable, they will supply the dis-

[11]U.S. Congress, Senate, Select Committee on Small Business, *An Analysis of Criminal Redistribution Systems and Their Impact on Small Business,* Staff Report, October 26, 1972, p. 7.

[12]U.S. Congress, *Criminal Redistribution (Fencing) Systems,* p. 2.

[13]*Ibid.,* pp. 144-56.

FIGURE 5-2
Channels of Distribution in the
Hijacking Connection

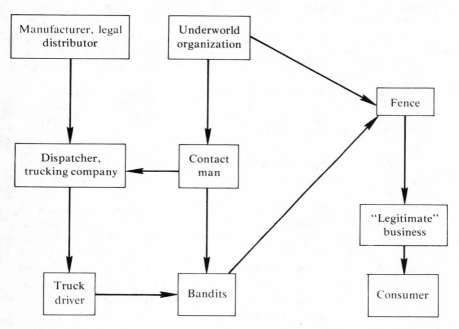

patcher with "front money"—often up to $10,000—to fix the contract. The dispatcher, in turn, will make arrangements with a truck driver to deliver the truck to a prearranged "drop."

Why would the driver cooperate with the dispatcher? Invariably, the dispatcher or another party would coerce or bribe the driver. For example, the driver might owe a gambling debt to a loan shark (who may also work for the dispatcher, contact man, or underworld), or he might be blackmailed for some indiscretion conveniently set up by those who desire his cooperation. The possibilities for manipulation are many. In any case, the driver may be willing to assist in the crime and when cross-examined will claim that he was "robbed by armed bandits." For his part, the driver is usually paid by the dispatcher from the front money.

After they receive the goods, the underworld managers dispose of them through the established fences. The fences, in turn, sell the goods to retailers or to other fences who ultimately sell to the consumer.

A third class of shadow system personnel includes shoplifters, price switchers, and petty thieves. Although each individual crime against a store may be for a trivial amount, it is estimated that shoplifters and price switchers extract amounts totaling approximately $3 billion and $100 million a year, respectively, from merchants. [14]

Supermarkets are particularly vulnerable to losses from these practices. Consider the following instances described in the *Wall Street Journal:*

> One Dallas grocer reports catching a customer carefully placing jumbo-sized eggs in a box for smaller ones in order to save nine cents on the box. Others say customers switch caps on pickle jars and ketchup bottles and shaving-cream cans.

> More serious are the shoppers creating bargains at the meat counter. A switcher might, for instance, take a two-pound roast and a five-pound roast out of a meat case, go to a deserted aisle, and painstakingly put the two-pound label on the five-pound roast. [15]

To combat these and other practices, merchants are using tamper-resistant tags and labels, increasing surveillance, and prosecuting many offenders.

On the selling side, there are also many petty practices by which the "commercial shadow battle" is expressed. Quite common, and accounting for an untold volume, are distortions in weights and measures, shortchanging, and overcharging at the checkout counter, in addition to bait and switch, and the variety of real and quasi-confidence games.

Illegal marketing practices are familiar the world around, including not only the many varieties of black market but also such tactics as the *nalevo* ("on the side") selling of goods and services in the USSR that is estimated to account for perhaps 50 percent of the economy. The widespread operation of the shadow system highlights the fact that "marketing" as ordinarily described by marketing textbooks is itself an expression of devotion to one value system. Most authors presuppose a relatively ideal, virtuous system predicated for the most part on legal forms of selling. The main deviations referred to are the milder aberrations of price collusion and other restraints of trade, plus the pressures against regulation that are often so lightly dismissed with consent decrees. Such textbooks usually overlook the *actual* functioning of a marketing system in which emotions of greed and indifference to precepts of equity and fair gain play a part, where consumer behavior includes elderly people stealing meat in desperation at its high price. Then, prices may be set not by the conventional seller at the markup he determines but by the "customer" who has decided on a markdown of his choosing, or by a "seller" whose main expense is front money and a warehouse for the drop.

---

[14]"Many Shoppers Find Some Real Bargains—By Switching Tags," *Wall Street Journal,* July 30, 1973, p. 1; *Criminal Redistribution (Fencing) Systems,* p. 2.

[15]*Wall Street Journal,* July 30, 1973, p. 1.

Social Marketing Conflict

Subjective, transactional, and competitive marketing conflict may be sorted out for separate attention, but they are of course interwoven in determining the offering, the taking, and the conditions of each marketing exchange. *Social marketing conflict* is also always present, implicitly or explicitly. It refers to *the encounter of differences in acceptability of the ideas and objects at issue to the social group.*

THE CONFLICT OVER ARRANGEMENTS

Social conflict may be seen as having two major elements of debate. The broadest has to do with determining what should be the fundamental structures of social arrangements—whether sociological, economic, political, legal, and so forth. When these possibilities are discussed theoretically, they tend to be the province of philosophers, economists, political scientists, legislators, editorial writers, and any citizens who interest themselves in such abstract topics. In such discourse, basic assertions are made about the nature of man, his basic needs, and how in some grand sense it is best for him to order his society and to relate to his environment.

These basic assertions and prescriptions are commonly dichotomized or polarized through the boldness or extremity of leaders' positions, so that one is either a realist or an idealist, an optimist or a pessimist, a Platonist or an Aristotelian. Many biologically oriented thinkers talk about the human as largely animal in nature, as an aggressive, territorial, naked ape. They market these views in works that are popular perhaps because some customers are comforted by the inference that one cannot be blamed for acting out greedy, aggressive, erotic, possessive impulses if Nature so ordains it. Ashley Montagu struggles, seemingly almost singlehandedly as the adversary reviewer, to refute the tide of animality unleashed by the simplifications of Robert Ardrey and Desmond Morris or the more sophisticated skills of Lionel Tiger and Robin Fox, or Konrad Lorenz, to maintain that people are basically good and loving.

In a more everyday vein is the conflict of ideas about the role of the individual in his society, and the constant adjustments that have to be made between what persons want and what the group should permit. Justified by philosophic position, religious directive, sociological analysis, psychological insight, or political power, society in general and subgroups within it arrive at crystallizations of ethical, moral, and legal sorts. For the time, laws, rules, and expectations guide people in how to feel, think, and act. But the dynamism of conflict continues to operate. The laws, rules, and expectations differ from group to group; "circumstances alter circumstances"; energies rise and fall; leaders come and go; and in the marketplace of ideas, groups contend for whose values shall predominate. They fashion their ideas and offer them to publics, exacting a price for adherence to them—and the publics buy the ideas by conforming to them, voting for them, urging legislation for them so that other people will have to buy them, willy-nilly; or they reject them, ignore them, refuse to obey them, vote against them, and offer alternatives.

Among the largest of issues is the arrangement of the economic system:

> In the view of some historians, the central conflict of the 20th Century is the struggle between the governments of nation states and private corporations to exercise power over economic fundamentals—land, human labor, materials, machines, money, markets.[16]

Spokesmen for the free-enterprise system laud its laissez-faire mechanisms for achieving (as John Davenport has said)[17] both freedom and order. In turn, those who favor central planning, or at least a substantial degree of it, and the controls that it requires, point to the inequities in society, and to the governmental assistance sought even by private corporations when they get into financial trouble. In a profit-and-loss system, it is supposed that people ought to be willing to be losers—but that idea may seem to exalt competitive efficiency and the price it exacts beyond what changing social values can tolerate. P. T. Bauer has argued that those who want to help developing countries with foreign aid in the belief that this is a rational means of improving their economic circumstances are actually expressing their guilt over Western prosperity.[18] He thinks that the flow of aid has inhibited rather than furthered the economic growth of the countries being paid, and that central planning in those countries has been a negative force. The value placed on self-reliance is reflected in the idea that the developed countries made it on their own, so to speak, and so should the developing ones.

Recognizing that some balance is realistically required, Walter Heller points toward the necessity of defining "much more sharply the optimum role of the federal government in its various fields of responsibility."[19] He cites Charles Shultz in differentiating the kinds of governmental provision that should be made: for example, direct income support to the aged, blind, and working poor; revenue sharing to local governments to reduce disparities; strings-attached monies to education and health services; medical care for the poor; and negative incentives to make pollution cost.

Not surprisingly, many of the discussions emphasizing the advantages of private enterprise are found in the *Wall Street Journal,* which echoes a broad

[16]"Public-Private Tensions," *Wall Street Journal,* August 16, 1973, p. 8.

[17]John A. Davenport, "Free Enterprise's Forgotten Virtues," *Wall Street Journal,* July 27, 1973, p. 8.

[18]P. T. Bauer, *Dissent on Development* (Boston: Harvard University Press, 1972).

[19]Walter Heller, "The Side-Effects of Nixon's Budget," *Wall Street Journal,* February 22, 1973, p. 14.

American perspective on this issue. Elsewhere, A. Dale Tussing analyzes various kinds of welfare systems, indicating how poor people are stigmatized and excluded because of this traditional outlook:

> No welfare programs are inherently legitimate in the United States where the dominant ideology of individualism still appears to reject the welfare state in principle (while applying it in practice—a conflict of some significance). In the view of many people, job-holders are members of and contributors to society; non-job-holders are not. [20]

Taking as his aim "the improvement of society and the general welfare," and on behalf of a constituency differing from that of the *Wall Street Journal,* Herbert Gans supports an income redistribution plan—a Credit Income Tax reform—that would dramatically affect the societal "sharing of the spoils" to which Lloyd Warner referred.[21]

THE CONTENDING GROUPS

As the foregoing examples imply, social marketing conflict is not merely a matter of competing ideologies. As with other entities in the marketplace the ideas have partisans, come from ideological entrepreneurs or sympathetic organizations, have salesmen who hawk them, and have media outlets suited to various marketing segments. Social marketing differs from competitive commercial marketing because the audience's response is not easily converted into monetary units that permit conventional calculation of gain and profit (although often money contributions are also sought). Social marketers seek to profit in other ways, to triumph in achieving (or moving toward) their goals of support, legislation, social change, against the groups in society that oppose these goals or prefer others.

In endless contention, the infinitely segmented population sustains these conflicts. No position is so virtuous in the eyes of all, so universally approved, that some others will not disagree with it, find it imperfect or evil, and seek to prevent its dominion. Thus many consumers are apathetic about efforts on their behalf, and some oppose consumer advocacy, finding the proposed cure worse than the disease.[22] Many women do not want the Equal Rights amendment passed, some blacks fight against busing, and so forth, indicating that every situation contains multiple values that can be emphasized to incline one in different directions. Intragroup conflict often seems self-defeating, yet the participants are driven by motives or pursuing interests that

[20]A. Dale Tussing, "The Dual Welfare System," *Society,* 11, No. 2 (January-February 1974), 50.

[21]Herbert Gans, "More Equality: Income and Taxes," *Society,* 11, No. 2 (January-February 1973), 63-69.

[22]Ralph Winter, Jr., *The Consumer Advocate versus the Consumer* (American Enterprise Institute, July 1972).

seem important to each. Harry Levinson shows how a family business can be riven by such differential perceptions and rivalries as classical intrafamilial emotions are acted out in the arena of the company. [23] In this instance, the conflict is simultaneously an example of intimate marketing, competitive marketing within an organization, and social marketing in the sense of involving larger policy issues such as the superiority of professional management.

When several groups are involved, the complexity of the issues is often impressive. In a report of Federal Trade Commission hearings on the Proposed Trade Regulation Rule to Preserve Consumers' Claims and Defenses, Karolin Blackson describes the positions taken by the various witnesses. These are listed as one representing the government, five professors—including one economist, a number of lawyers representing business interests, banks, finance companies, and credit-card operators, as well as automobile dealers, plus six consumer representatives and an advocate of the National Consumer Act. Blackson summarizes:

> It was evident from the testimony given during the extensive hearings that many individuals and industries have strong feelings on the subject. Generally, the representatives from affected industries took exception to some of the provisions in the proposed revised rule; on the other hand, those who work directly with low-income consumers took the position that the proposed rule would be of immeasurable assistance to them in aiding consumers who used credit unwisely. [24]

MARKETING CONFLICTS WITH THE LARGER SOCIETY

A widely held view of commercial marketing is that while it is a major force in society, it generally operates antagonistically to the interests of society. A number of value issues are implicit or explicit in the arguments put forward by supporters of this view. Several of these value issues will be presented here.

One general issue is that the conceptions of the desirable are basically different for professional marketers and nonprofessional marketers. Professional marketers stress and perpetuate materialistic goals as opposed to more spiritual goals. "Commercialization of Christmas" in the religious arena and "profit from misery" in family planning are examples of charges that imply that marketers somehow are subverting some higher-order values, such as spiritual well-being and altruism.

[23]Harry Levinson, "Conflicts That Plague Family Businesses," *Harvard Business Review,* March-April 1971, pp. 90-98.

[24]Karolin Blackson, "Preservation of Consumers' Claims and Defenses," *Consumer Credit Leader,* 2, No. 10 (May 1973), 4-26.

Another related issue is that marketing reallocates the scarce resources of both the firm and the consumer (and hence society) from key problem areas found in health, education, and welfare to activities of marginal importance to society. As one critic of marketing put it, "If all the money spent on hamburgers at MacDonald's by low income families was spent purchasing the same commodity at a cooperative supermarket the average level of nutrition among these families would improve by fifteen percent." Hamburger stands are thus cast as obstacles to the improvement of the nutritional well-being of certain groups of consumers. Similarly it is charged that money spent advertising highly marginal differences between otherwise identical products could be more usefully spent on day-care centers and so forth. The basic charge here is that marketers do not focus their efforts upon key societal problems and, indeed, thwart the solution of these problems.

A refinement of the charge just mentioned is that marketers use undue guile in pursuing their interests, by inappropriately identifying their goods and services with so-called higher-order social objectives or values. The brand name of a fruit juice may imply a higher vitamin content than is in fact the case. Some children's games have been cited as claiming in their advertising an educational impact far beyond what can be objectively demonstrated. Thus, it is argued, marketers in some cases unduly identify their products with important social values, such as health or physical well-being and education.

Some critics of marketing claim that second-order consequences of marketing, that is, consequences beyond those intended, are ignored by marketers. The effects of child-oriented advertising upon parent-child relationships are a supposed instance of this. Still another is the litter on streets and highways, abandoned cars, and so forth, as the result of overpromotion resulting in overconsumption which results in the careless discarding of waste. Another commonly noted second-order consequence (although not generally phrased as such) is the supposed excess expenditure of funds on promotion. As competitive goods and services multiply, it is necessary to increase advertising and other forms of sales promotion. Such increases in sales promotion, it is argued, increase the cost of goods sold and hence raise prices to the ultimate consumer. The conclusion is then drawn that the business value of profit maximization is in conflict with the general welfare values of society.

Charges are also made that marketing neglects the consumer value of reasonable choice. At one end of the issue are critics who argue that consumer choice preferences are not taken into account in the development of the firm's product mix. This assumes an excessive orientation to the sales concept. At the other end of the issue are those who argue that consumers have too many alternatives to choose from in satisfying some need and hence cannot make fully informed decisions. This, perhaps, assumes an excessive orientation to the marketing concept. In either case, the basic criticism is that there is an abridgement of the consumer's right to make reasoned, unencumbered choice decisions.

Another value that marketers are charged with violating is the *right* of the consumer *to know* the ultimate objectives of particular marketing activities or strategies directed at the consumer. Perhaps the most frequently cited violation of this right is the bait-and-switch ploy described in Chapter 4. A customer is encouraged to visit a store on the basis of a low-price offering for a particularly desired product. Once the customer is in the store, the salesman tries to switch him to a higher-priced alternative. This is often facilitated in the case of appliances and other durable goods by having only one product at that price. The product is likely to sell quickly, and subsequent customers find the advertised item out of stock and thus are more likely to purchase a higher-priced item. It is claimed that if stock is limited or only one single item is available, then this must be made clear in the promotion to the customer.

VALUE CONFLICTS AMONG MARKETERS

The marketing profession itself is a social system, and there are many sources of value conflict. The emphasis here is upon conflict between marketing consultants and their clients. Virtually everything that is said about this relationship is applicable to the relationship between marketing managers and personnel within their span of control.

It may seem strange at first to think that sufficient conflict or potential conflict may exist between marketing consultants and their clients to warrant discussion. This perspective is particularly likely to arise among those who still cling to the notion of value-free science and total objectivity among its practitioners. Indeed, values color all decisions made by, and actions taken by, marketers—and by theoretical high energy physicists too, for that matter. The important questions to ask are, "Whose side are you on?" and "Do you know it?" In the discussion that follows we shall highlight some of the areas and issues where value conflicts are likely to arise between marketing consultant and client.

Compatibility of Marketing Consultant and Client System Goals. The goals of the marketing consultant and the client system may or may not coincide. This depends in part upon the level of goals under discussion. For example, a management consultant may be concerned with maximizing his financial gain derived from serving as a consultant. This goal or concern may not be compatible with the client system's desire to limit the outflow of financial resources in all areas of activity. At the same time, both a consultant and a client system place high value on improving the marketing performance of the organization in one or more areas. For the consultant, this increases the likelihood of being rehired in the future.

The issue involved here is quite thorny. There are several questions. Must the client or the client system disclose to the consultant the nature of the goals that the consultant's advice is intended to further? Must a consultant be told that his services will be used to develop an advertising campaign stressing appeals he feels socially undesirable? Should a marketing channels specialist be informed that a family-planning clinic or health delivery system he is helping to design is going to emphasize a birth-control technique to which he is opposed by virtue of his religion or other value considerations? Similarly, should the client be fully informed of the values of the consultant? This is particularly important if there is any danger that the means for furthering goals can alter those goals and that the consultant, with values at variance with those of the client, may unwittingly make recommendations that will tend to subvert those goals.

Imposition of Interventionist's Values. One of the first questions that can be raised is whether the marketing consultant is aware that he is acting on the basis of certain values and that he is not engaging in an activity in a value-free way. There is the very important issue of what values and therefore whose values are to be served by the consultancy. There is a natural tendency for the consultant to promulgate his values. In such circumstances we must ask whether these values are representative of those possessed by the client. Often the answer is yes because clients tend to seek out interventionists with like value schemes. But sometimes the marketing consultant may discover only belatedly that a discrepancy in values exists between himself and the client. For example, in a specific situation the client who selects the consultant may not always share the values of the larger system or of key colleagues and may call in a consultant known by the client to be sympathetic to his view. The consultant is used selectively, and possibly unknowingly so, by the client while the marketing consultant may be assuming the client is representative of all members of the firm.

In general, questions can also be raised as to which of the marketing consultant's values are most relevant to the activities he is to perform. These activities may include problem definition, program planning, implementation, evaluation, and control. It is likely that different values are differentially relevant to different activities. For example, values concerning the use of fear appeals may be most relevant for promotional-planning problems, whereas values concerning the rights of human subjects may be most relevant when the marketing consultant is conducting research as part of the problem diagnosis process.

Selection of Clients. Is a professional marketing consultant obligated to provide assistance to anyone who requests it? Can he refuse his services to clients whose values are not compatible with his own? In the legal and particularly in the medical sectors of society, the answer to this is fairly easy and clear: mechanisms do exist for providing these services to persons or groups who can demonstrate a need for legal and medical services and the inability to satisfy their need in conventional ways. It is also clear that vendors of restaurant services, real estate, and other commodities and services cannot refuse clients on the basis of certain values, such as those associated with the desire or preference not to have blacks or families with children as neighbors or customers. This issue of selecting and refusing services is likely to become more salient as social action agencies increasingly direct their requests for assistance to marketers.

Nature of Marketing Research Contract. The contract established between the client system and the consultant can be complex, and there may be several key issues that are not addressed in the contract. Who is the client? Is it the manager who brought the consultant into the organization, or is it the organization as a whole? Does the unit to be most directly affected by the consultant's efforts act as a group in seeking his help, or are there just certain key members of that group who seek his help? How are conflicts in values and approaches to the problem to be solved? Is the consultant free to opt out when he feels an unsolvable conflict exists? How responsible is the consultant for dysfunctional effects of his efforts? Should he make his services available to dealing with unforeseen problems of a solution after its implementation, or does his responsibility simply end after a solution is implemented?

Type of Intervention. The choice of means to implement change represents another important area where value and ethical dilemmas are likely to arise for marketing consultants. There are many strategies or types of intervention. These have been classified as coercive, persuasive, educative, and facilitative. *Manipulation* has been defined as " . . . [the] deliberate act of changing either the structure of the alternatives in the environment . . . or personal qualities affecting choice without the knowledge of the person involved . . ."[25] If manipulation is defined in this fashion, then all strategies involve manipulation to some extent. A marketing consultant is always related to manipulation, as when he provides information for sales managers to use in deciding where, when, and how to reorganize sales territories or sales quotas among salesmen.

Thus manipulation is not a phenomenon that can be sidestepped by the consultant who may claim that he only provided information or advice. Nor can it be sidestepped by the client who may claim that it was the consultant who by word or deed produced some change. The former case assumes a value-free activity in presenting particular information or recommendations to the client. The latter case, at the very least, assumes no value bias in the selection of a consultant and in the cooperation provided him. Neither assumption seems tenable.

We certainly agree with the Population Task Force of the Institute of Society, Ethics and the Life Sciences that core values such as *freedom* (the

---

[25]Donald Warwick and Herbert Kelman, "Ethical Issues in Social Intervention" in *Processes and Phenomena of Social Change,* Gerald Zaltman, ed. (New York: Wiley Interscience, 1973), p. 403.

capacity, opportunity, and incentive to make and act on reflective choices), *justice* (equitable distribution of rewards and punishments), and *welfare* (maintenance and improvement of vital interests of society) should be preserved. Inevitably, however, matters of interpretation arise. Consider the sales manager whose own position would be enhanced if a particular redesign of sales territories was put into effect producing more revenue for the firm and certain salesmen, yet less income for other salesmen. The redesign and reallocation of sales territories—say, giving more effective salesmen more or better territory—is consistent with the welfare of the manager, the firm, and certain salesmen. At the same time it is not to the welfare of still other salesmen who lose by the change. It can be argued that it is only justice being done by rewarding those who sell more effectively and punishing those who do not. But this is a value position unique to certain cultures.

Responsibility for Diagnosing the Problem. Before discussing some of the issues involved in the responsibility for the outcome of change efforts, it is necessary to pause and consider the diagnosis of the problem. In many ways, the diagnosis of marketing problems determines the general outline of the solution(s) and in this indirect way is related to the change outcome. To the extent that problem definition and change outcome are related, the issue of responsibility for the outcomes is partly rooted in the responsibility for the problem definition. It would seem that the marketing consultant's responsibilities for the outcomes of his recommendation vary as partial functions of his involvement in the problem definition. The same reasoning is applicable to his involvement in the various activities related to the implementation of change strategies.

There seems to be little discussion in the literature as to how an individual's values affect his diagnosis of problems. In general, values influence both the stimuli to which one attends and the interpretation and weighting of the corresponding data. A consultant who places high value on educational appeals in advertising is particularly likely to look for and notice the extent to which educational appeals are used relative to overtly persuasive appeals. He is more apt to be critical of a perceived emphasis on persuasive appeals and to rate this perceived emphasis as an important factor contributing to poor response to promotional efforts.

The client is also a value-laden social unit. Values of the client, for example, determine the selection of information to be given to the marketing consultant for evaluation. Moreover, client values may cause a particular structuring of information that presents a biased view as to the nature and source of problems. This raises the general issue of how much freedom the consultant has in discovering what he would define as the real problem. The withholding of information from a consultant restricts the number of alternative problems he is able to identify and choose from. In this special sense his freedom of choice has been narrowed. His freedom of choice is further narrowed if the data provided him are highly structured in a certain way so that certain interpretations are unlikely. Thus an important operating strategy for the consultant is to consider the client's definition, if any, of the problem as a hypothesis. The consultant's first task, then, is to collect his own data in the system to determine if in fact the client's definition of the problem is suitable or reasonable. Of critical importance here is the consultant's access to information. The consultant must be allowed to gather the information he feels is needed to fulfill his role.

One issue not yet mentioned concerns value conflicts between the interventionist and the client in determining the means of implementing a solution. One position on this issue is that the consultant is obligated to discuss such conflict with the client. It is also considered entirely appropriate, however, for the consultant to be as partisan and persuasive as he chooses. It should be noted that the consultant cannot be expected to know *a priori* how his values may differ from those of the client. If the client or some third party initiates the contact leading to a consulting relationship, the interventionist may well mistakenly assume that there is compatibility in basic values.

Once a problem solution or a change is implemented, the issue of responsibility for its impact becomes important. With respect to the marketing consultant and his client, there are several important issues. Once a change has been implemented, what responsibility does the consultant have for the unintended dysfunctional consequences that may result? Is the consultant required to provide services to the client to help resolve these dysfunctional consequences, or is it no longer the consultant's responsibility? For example, the introduction of a marketing information system may pose a threat to some managers in the system with the result that they are very resistant to its use. Should the marketing consultant who introduced this MIS be required to come back and help the client system reduce this resistance, or is this totally someone else's responsibility? One might make the case that if the consultant had been more sensitive to resistance to change, he might have introduced the MIS in a way that would reduce the resistance of those affected.

The issue of responsibility also applies to the client. In the MIS example, the same issue of responsibility can be raised. What responsibility does the client system have in helping people deal with the psychological impact of change? Should the client system be sensitive and supportive of those affected by the change? Beyond helping people deal with the psychological impact of change, what responsibility does the client system have for relocating personnel who may be displaced as a result of the introduction of some technological change?

SPECIFIC INTERGROUP ISSUES

One of the issues of concern in the society has to do with how people should be permitted to communicate with each other in order to engage in commercial marketing. Some communities prohibit door-to-door solicitation—those potential customers who would not mind it having lost the battle, possibly not even having been directly party to the deliberations that produced the ordinance. Certain kinds of mail may not be sent to citizens who have requested that their names be removed from the mailing list.

THE CONFLICT OVER ADVERTISING

Perhaps no single aspect of marketing raises the ire of consumers, businessmen, government officials, and others as does advertising. The arguments of those for and against advertising are complex and do not fall into discrete categories. However, for purposes of analysis, it is possible to identify specific actions and reactions, particular protagonists and antagonists, and related phenomena associated with the inherent conflictual nature of advertising processes.

Government versus Advertisers. That advertising elicits simultaneous reactions of attraction and repulsion is well illustrated in the case of government relations. On the one hand, the government (in the form of the legislature, the courts, and the FTC) considers restricting advertising through such measures as the Truth-in-Advertising Act or proposed guidelines for commercials directed at children. On the other hand, numerous federal, state, and local agencies spend millions of dollars each year on advertisements connected with their operations. The navy, for example, planned an advertising budget of $24.9 million for fiscal 1974. [26]

The dialogue between government (as critic) and advertisers centers around three fundamental issues: (1) the role of advertising, (2) the characteristics of advertising, and (3) the effects or consequences of advertising. Each category overlaps and interacts with the others to produce the complexity of issues and positions.

Typically, critics and proponents view the *role of advertising* from diverse perspectives. To the critic, ideal advertising is regarded in a narrow, neutral sense. That is, the sole function of advertising is to make available information to consumers of product or service offerings so that they may make intelligent choices with a minimum of effort. This role is usually defined and limited to providing price, availability, and other functional information. It is a relatively passive outlook in the sense that advertisers cannot persuade or influence consumers by using embellishments, psychological or other "noninformational" appeals, but must rely on the consumer's perceived image of a limited range of physical attributes. This viewpoint has led the government to enact or propose such restrictions as truth-in-lending and truth-in-advertising bills, cooling-off laws, and unit-pricing guidelines.

[26] John Revett, "Recruit Ads under Review by Defense Dept. Execs.," *Advertising Age,* May 7, 1973.

To the advertising proponent, advertising has a multiple role. In addition to providing information, advertising is a form of promotion with the frequent explicit objective of influencing consumers to want and purchase a particular product. It is a central mechanism of competition among many sellers which claims to result in better products and services. To restrict advertising to informational appeals, the proponents argue, is to reduce competition between sellers and hence adversely affect consumer welfare.

The government and the advertisers also differ in regard to their perception of existing *characteristics of advertising.* From the perspective of various government agencies, advertising is often both deceptive and fraudulent in its actions. A major source of the government's information comes from irate consumers who, for example, send up to two thousand complaints or inquiries per month to the President's Office of Consumer Affairs.[27] In contrast, advertisers define so-called distortion and embellishment as legitimate (and inherently inevitable) techniques for persuasion, while wrongdoing "consists only of falsification with larcenous intent." [28] Thus the government assumes a broad definition of deception which includes all distortion, and advertisers advocate a stricter definition of deception which excludes "distortion" as a slippery and ambiguous concept.

Not only is there disagreement on what constitutes deception, but the government and the advertisers vary in their preferences for enforcement. As one might expect, the government prefers laws, regulations, and guidelines explicitly specifying what behaviors can and cannot be condoned. Advertisers on the other hand, regard such restrictions as unnecessary and harmful to competition and prefer individual responsibility and self-regulation.

Government critics and the defenders of advertising differ considerably with respect to conceptions of the *consequences of advertising.* To the critic, advertising leads to materialism, manipulation, and an ineffective economy. To the advertising defender, advertising produces more good than harm.

Advertising is often criticized for its role in controlling human behavior. It is credited with the creation of a "materialistic mentality," as well as overt manipulation in the marketplace. Moreover, by making it necessary to advertise extensively in order to compete, advertising adversely affects competition and raises artificial barriers to entry.[29]

The advertising advocate counters with a number of arguments. First, the positive consequences of advertising are thought to far outweigh the negative. With respect to materialism, such beneficial effects as the increased standard of living, freedom for leisure, improved longevity and health, and generally enhanced quality of life are all cited as net gains due, in part, to advertising.

[27]Myrna Blyth, "Knauer Power," *Family Health,* 4 (May 1972), 18*ff.*

[28]Theodore Levitt, "Morality (?) of Advertising," *Harvard Business Review,* July 1970, p. 85.

[29]See Reed Moyer, *Macro Marketing: A Social Perspective* (New York: John Wiley & Sons, Inc., 1972), Chap. 2.

Second, the charge of manipulation is denied. The vast majority of psychological research indicates that the limits of persuasion are considerable, and people are sophisticated in their ability to "turn off," counterargue, and question that which does not agree with their values and wants. [30] It may even be argued that advertising can reduce manipulations by allowing the consumer to choose from among many competitors who, in the long run, must satisfy consumers if they are to survive. Finally, the evidence with respect to advertising's effect on barriers to entry is inconclusive. While some maintain that advertising can contribute to increased concentration ratios and possibly lessen competition, [31] others stress that many new producers enter the market each year and compete successfully. [32] The analysis is complicated by the fact that product differentiation, economies of scale, and nonpricing marketing strategies interact with advertising.

Consumers show an array of attitudes toward advertising, also, paralleling those found in the institutional forces already noted. Most generally, consumers are quite tolerant of advertising, taking it largely for granted as a part of the environment. They pay attention to a great number of advertising communications, learn much from them, and use them in various ways. They relate to different forms of advertising without making formal or precise distinctions between them. For example, they are quite positive about magazine advertising, often maintaining that the advertising content is as important if not more so than the editorial content of the magazine. Newspaper advertising is used heavily for immediate information about current products and prices, as well as to reinforce concepts of products, brands, and retail outlets. [33]

Along with this general attitude of casual acceptance is a willingness to be critical of advertising, to follow the leadership of consumerist spokesmen, to support Ralph Nader. Because of the tendency to equate advertising and marketing with their most negative manifestations, they are easily lambasted.

Major sources of criticism of advertising are its obvious self-seeking character, its insistence on asserting itself with interruptions if necessary, and the sense of greed and pettiness that seems inherent in urging people to buy. Even when people desire the goods, and the messages are innocuous, they are vulnerable to seeming unnecessary to free choice, as consumers are usually unaware of how unavailable many things would be if they were not advertised.

[30] *Ibid.*, pp. 46-47.

[31] Louis W. Stern and Thomas W. Dunfee, "Public Policy Implications of Non-price Marketing and De-oligopolization in the Cereal Industry," in *Public Policy and Marketing Practices,* ed. Fred Allvine (Chicago: American Marketing Association, 1973), pp. 285-86.

[32] Jules Backman, *Advertising and Competition* (New York: New York University Press, 1967), pp. 42-51, 68.

[33] Charles B. McCann, *Women and Department Store Newspaper Advertising* (Chicago: Social Research, Inc., 1957).

The contention among various positions is bound to be continuous, as they are based on incompatible assumptions and values. One position says people should be given information so they can make knowledgeable choices. The implication is that people know what they want and what is best for themselves, or can figure this out, if advertising gives just the facts. Others feel this is an illusion of objectivity, as it is often not clear what the facts are or which are relevant, and an advertisement cannot give them all. In addition, those who object to advertising that is "solely informative," including both producers and receivers of it, say it is dull, and more of it would produce a flood of information impossible to deal with, more suited to technical manuals than to advertisements.

Another avenue to the supposedly autonomous consumer is to assume that since he knows what he wants—at some level in his psyche—rather than give him more information than he can assimilate, it is better to study his needs and wants and to gratify them. An opposing value system claims that the consumer's needs and wants are generally mediocre and, if catered to, result in general debasement of taste and of the culture. Thus, in the social conflicts that go on in the society around the issues of advertising, the consumers are varied voices responding to and criticizing advertising and at the same time are pawns in the struggle between those who want to give consumers what they want and those who believe advertisers have a duty to elevate public taste. Both problems are further compounded when the former have difficulty figuring out what consumers "really" do want and the latter cannot agree on what the elevating experiences should be.

Some further examples of contemporary issues are useful to highlight the way various groups interact in the continuous flux whereby old groups war over new issues and new groups spring up to fight old issues.

Complicating the traditional conflicts of labor versus management has been the conversion of labor into labor unions. This classic confrontation is often triangular, with both unions and management competing for the co-operation or loyalty of the workers. The issue of job enrichment in some form or other, from the good working conditions that distinguished the H. J. Heinz Company at the turn of the century to the insights gained from the Western Electric Hawthorne plant studies in the twenties and to the current idea of being able to "manage" one's own work, has provoked labor unions as being a distraction from bread-and-butter issues. *The Wall Street Journal* comments on the modern conflict:

> It also seems inevitable that the clashing objectives of union leaders and job enrichment advocates herald an intensifying battle for the hearts of the nation's workers, both organized and unorganized. That the workers are receptive to both job enrichment and higher pay is documented in a recent survey by pollster Louis Harris.
>
> Mr. Harris found that some 64% of the workers questioned would be "very willing to work harder" if their pay were increased. An almost identical per-

centage, 61% said they'd work harder if they had "more say" about the kind of work they did and the way they did it.

The normal union-management adversary relationship is an abrasive one at best, and the coming struggle may well make it more so. [34]

The shift in the relative emphasis placed on wages and hours relates to changing concepts of the nature of the worker, his dignity, his use of leisure, his need for amenities; with greater affluence and education, his self-concept changes and he insists on being dealt with in new ways. He markets himself differently from the way he did in the past, may generally be fussier about what he will do—and even if he will go to work or not on any given day. In his intimate marketing the working-class man changes in his willingness to give his family more time, in his commercial marketing he may outspend less prosperous middle-class people, and in his social marketing he broadens his horizons to include more civic participation.

Unions and management in a sense compete for the worker's mind. Such competition in the sphere of social marketing is widespread. Contention for the minds of children is another issue in society, as various groups seek to sell their views concerning who should be allowed to communicate to children, in what settings, with what intentions. As in all marketing, these questions basically ask what product or service should be provided, how it should be promoted, whose labors should be rewarded, and so forth. This struggle goes on over schooling, with much debate over the efficacy of the product offered there, [35] and over day-care services, busing, books, and movies, to say nothing of advertising.

THE BATTLE FOR THE MINDS OF CHILDREN

Children occupy a special status in society as characterized by the preferential treatment and care they receive in family as well as in institutional relationships. It is no wonder, then, that the subject of advertising directed at children generates volatile reactions and sharp differences of opinion.

On the one hand, advertisers—and marketers in general—view children as a legitimate market worthy of their efforts. On the other hand, members of the Federal Trade Commission and of the Department of Health, Education, and Welfare, irate parents, and various consumer groups view child-oriented advertising as an insidious intrusion into vulnerable lives. [36]

[34] *Wall Street Journal,* February 26, 1973, p. 10.

[35] Ivan Illich, *Deschooling Society* (New York: Harper & Row, Publishers, 1971); Christopher Jencks *et al., Inequality* (New York: Basic Books, Inc., Publishers, 1973); and Colin Greer, *The Great School Legend* (New York: Basic Books, Inc., Publishers, 1972).

[36] Attitudes toward children's commercials are part of the more general views held about television advertising. For an extended discussion of the complexities of these views, see Chapter 9, "The Love and Fear of Commercials," in Ira O. Glick and Sidney J. Levy, *Living with Television* (Chicago: Aldine Publishing Company, 1962), pp. 204-28.

The attacks on advertising range from demands to ban all television advertising directed at children (a position advocated by the consumer group Action for Children's Television, ACT) to the more moderate posture of the FTC calling for special protection from "unfair practices." Typically, the charges are that television advertising manipulates or coerces children, creates reality-fantasy distortions, encourages disruptive parent-child relationships, and unduly fashions attitudes, values, and desires.[37]

The charges of manipulation have been voiced most strongly by the ACT group, which maintains that "sophisticated advertising techniques are often used to deceive, cajole, and exploit the youngest and least knowledgeable members of our society."[38] In these critics' views, the impact of television is seen to be too influential, if not actually irresistible.

Advertising is also attacked for its effects on the parent-child relationship. The logic is that the child is seduced by the advertising to want the product and then plays a marketing role vis-à-vis the parents in urging them to buy it.

> . . . the purpose [of advertising] is to use the child as a surrogate salesman to pressure the parent into buying the product. This is unfair to the child . . . this is unfair to the parent . . . and this can be damaging to the parent-child relationship." [Action for Children's Television]

•   •   •

> The child, then, is put in the position of an inexperienced solicitor; and the parent, an experienced though unsolicited buyer. When the parent denies the child's request for an advertised product he may feel guilty or resentful at being repeatedly placed in the position of having to say "no." [Frederick C. Green, Department of Health, Education, and Welfare]

In contrast, the defenses of advertising range from outright denial of any negative effects to the position that children receive a number of benefits from advertising. In one formal statement, marketers counter by emphasizing that advertising may have useful socializing results. That is, children may learn the role of consumption in their lives, and through interactions with their parents, they may achieve more competence in coping with the "realities of independent living."

> We suggest that the social justification for advertising to children arises from the process of consumer socialization—experience as a purchaser—both in its own right and as a training ground for other types of decision-making. A significant test of maturity is the ability to make reasonably good choices and decisions in a wide variety of circumstances. We believe that the discussion children have with their parents about product purchases as a result of exposure to

---

[37]Thomas S. Robertson, "The Impact of Television Advertising on Children," *Wharton Quarterly*, Fall 1972, pp. 38-41.

[38]*Ibid.*, p. 38. See also Carol Andreas, "War Toys and the Peace Movement," *Journal of Social Issues*, 25, No. 1 (1969), 83-99.

[39]Robertson, *op. cit.*, p. 40.

advertising, as well as experience with actual purchases, contributes to maturation. Involved in this long and painful process (but no more so than other maturation processes) is the learning of the proper criteria to use in evaluating products, the value of money spent now for several small items versus the purchase of a larger item later, the determination of the standards appropriate to a particular age, class and way of life, and finally, the development of character . . . In addition to the creation of self-confidence, the child learns to know what he himself wants. Knowledge of one's self arises from experience in making decisions and knowing their ultimate results.[40]

Many parents agree with this basic position. These parents notice that their children pay attention to commercials, believe they are learning about the real world of the marketplace, and are proud of the cognitive skills they may display. The argument implies that parents who want to deprive their children of television commercials directed at them are seeking to evade constructive vigorous interactions with their children and would deprive them of important experiences, presumably even with products viewed as good or commercials that are not deceptive. By making marketing decisions *for* children who would not be receiving commercial instruction in wanting and arguing for advertised products, family life would perhaps be calmer, with parents feeling less guilty about saying no, but children would be denied chances for enhancing their personal growth.

Within these opposing positions are at least two main views of society. The ACT and HEW positions cited imply a society in which parents (and the surrogates they may accept, such as the school) have the greater strength—the child is not reinforced in pressuring the parents. Forces outside the family are to be excluded from introducing their pressures for demands, changes, new choices, and the family can continue in its traditional ways. Toys priced at $27.95 may exist, or toy weapons, but should not be permitted to make their attractive presence known to impressionable children—impressions should be controlled by the superior judgments of the elders. Of course, the extremity of the position is relative: if only children's commercials were to be banned, children would have sufficient exposure to other selling messages and the commercialism of modern society (and would undoubtedly learn that weapons are highly valued by millions of Americans).

The advertising position says that in our society alluring, expensive products exist and that children capable of realizing it should not be protected from that knowledge or the knowledge that the family may not be able to afford them. No advertiser argues publicly for distortion or falsehood. On the contrary, for example, the Tatham-Laird & Kudner agency, in a piece of promotional literature on its philosophy, expresses its responsibility to "so act and to so prepare advertising that the stature of advertising, the stature of the agency and the goodwill of its clients will not be jeopardized by questions

[40]Seymour Banks, quoted in J. Robert Moskin, ed., *The Case For Advertising* (American Association of Advertising Agencies, 1973), p. 52.

of truth, intent or taste." But these latter questions are not easily defined or agreed upon. Some people maintain (Levitt, e.g.) that room must be left for the usual human modes of expressiveness—that it is unreasonable to expect advertising to be devoid of fantasy, hyperbole, excitement, color, and implication, and thus to conform to a literalness hardly to be found anywhere else in society.

Another defense of advertising and agency practice is predicated on the value of trying to help people to achieve their ends. Aligning itself on the side of reinforcement of existing attitudes and desires, it asserts the essence of the "marketing concept." One spokesman for this defense is Dr. Banks of the Leo Burnett agency:

> We conduct research among children to develop advertising and products based on determining children's needs and desires. We do not attempt to alter them through advertising but, rather we alter advertising to be compatible with the existing child attitudes.[41]

Since there are various kinds of children with various needs and desires, and what reinforces one market segment may be persuasive or provocative to another, there is a problem in using media that reach more than one segment. But this overlap is inevitable, so that the earlier character-building argument for exposure to choices is required.

The differences in opinion on the issues of advertising to children are far from resolved. And most positions are not well supported by research on the effects of advertising on children.[42] Lewis Engman, chairman of the FTC, suggests eight problem areas to be considered in a voluntary code for the regulation of television advertising:

1. Use of visual techniques that distort product performance with regard to speed, time, motion, or size.
2. Confusion over sale price or accessories included in price.
3. Encouraging purchase of food items, particularly soft drinks, candy and snacks, without saying how they fit into a well balanced nutrition program.
4. Use of premiums and contests to create artificial demands.
5. The "surrogate salesman"—the use of children to suggest that parents buy or use a product.
6. Exposing children to products known to affect mood or sense of well-being.
7. Use of program characters to sell to children.
8. Use of material which creates anxiety or encourages safe acts.[43]

[41]*Ibid.*, p. 52.

[42]See Lewis A. Berey and Richard W. Pollay, "The Influencing Role of the Child in Family Decision Making," *Journal of Marketing Research,* 5 (February 1968), 70-72; Scott Ward and Thomas S. Robertson, "Family Influences on Adolescent Consumer Behavior," *First Annual Conference, Association for Consumer Research,* Amherst, Mass., August 1970; Scott Ward, Thomas S. Robertson, and Daniel Wackman, "Children's Attention to Television Advertising," in *Proceedings Association for Consumer Research,* ed. David M. Gardner, 1971, pp. 143-56; Thomas S. Robertson and John R. Rossiter, "Children and Commercial Persuasion: An Attribution Theory Analysis," *Journal of Consumer Research,* 1, No. 1 (June 1974).

[43]Stanley E. Cohen, "FTC Plans Industry Meeting to Set Children's TV Ad Rules," *Advertising Age,* August 6, 1973, p. 1.

The controversial aspects of these issues are manifold, especially when the consequences likely to ensue from attempts to implement their implied recommendations are considered. The inhibition of freedom they all imply is modified by Engman's reluctance to make them involuntary. The problems of definition are great, to which may be added the absurdities in trying so closely to control the possibilities for perceptual distortions, confusions, and anxieties, and distinguishing an "artificial demand" from any other. Before these issues can be solved, probably the more fundamental ones need to be addressed: of the conflict between social values of protecting children and overprotecting them, of expressiveness versus literalness in communication, of where the controls will be applied—in law, family interaction, the marketplace.

From abstractions about the nature of man, through debate over the structure of society, its social policies, and its larger institutions and processes such as education, advertising, and the nature of work, there is constant translation of these issues into products. Then the products may become the issues, being transformed from social marketing issues into commercial marketing practices. Controversies over kinds of school environments become construction trade activities and arguments over buildings, and something like the New Math can make some textbooks obsolete and others a great success.

SELLING MORALLY CONTROVERSIAL PRODUCTS AND SERVICES

All marketing conflict has a moral element in that those who criticize the seller or the buyer of anything they disapprove are likely to feel morally justified and righteous about their position. Whether the consequences are an illegal distribution system or just children nagging their parents for expensive toys, if the marketing is thought to be wrong, it becomes morally controversial. However, some products and services are more specifically and directly regarded as morally controversial, and views about what is good for the community or for the individual then find intense expression in conflicts between and among sellers and buyers. The WCTU and the Right to Life organizations, for example, actively oppose the selling of alcoholic beverages and abortion services, respectively. Other conflicts are diffused among individual consumers and marketers, resulting in bad-mouthing, gossip, or various latent forms of discontent. Table 5-1 lists a number of current controversial products and services available in many markets. In each instance a demand exists for these items, there are those who provide them, and there are those who seek actively to prevent the availability and use of such things.

In many instances the conflict is in a high state of tension and change. In the United States, until recently, those who wanted to have an abortion had to leave the country, or meet stringent local legal conditions, or search for an underground source. Unfortunately, the third option was not only illegal and

TABLE 5-1

Some Morally Controversial Products and Services

Contraceptives	Sunday selling
Pornography	Twenty-four-hour selling
Family-planning information	Student research and term papers
Abortion services	Alcoholic beverages
Cigarettes	Animal fur coats, leather, meat
Firearms	Phosphate detergents
Nonreturnable bottles	Lotteries
Horse race mutuels	Gold
Firecrackers	

often expensive, it entailed considerable risk to the life of the woman because those performing such operations were often unskilled or careless fugitives hiding in the shadow system. The increased demand from certain segments of the public, coupled with legal and legislative pressures by such groups as the National Organization of Women, led to the relaxation of restrictions against abortion and a favorable decision by the Supreme Court legalizing the practice. Yet the battles between those pro and con are far from over. A number of groups continue to oppose abortion and press for legislative change. They harass, sue, and picket clinics and medical centers.

> . . . they are well-organized. The hard core consists mainly of educated Catholics—doctors, lawyers, teachers and nurses—who are attracting a wider following, by no means all of which is Catholic. Activists include Republicans and Democrats, veterans of the anti-war and civil-rights movements and a host of otherwise unaffiliated middle-class Americans. As a consequence of all this, national politicians as well as legislators are beginning to take them seriously, and they threaten to mount a real challenge to the newly formulated right of abortion.[44]

A similar continuing conflict goes on over pornography, its definition, to what extent it should be permitted in the community, and how its control contravenes the First Amendment.[45]

Controversies such as these pose dilemmas to marketers. Should an advertiser accept an account to market products or services that—though sought by some—are opposed by others?[46] Whose values should be taken into account in any marketing effort? The target consumer's, the marketer's the other group's, the general public's? How may marketers decide whether a

[44]Jeffrey A. Tannenbaum, "Many Americans Join Move to Ban Abortion: Legislatures Take Note," *Wall Street Journal,* August 2, 1973, p. 1.

[45]W. Cody Wilson, "Pornography: The Emergence of a Social Issue and the Beginning of Psychological Study," *Journal of Social Issues,* 29, No. 3 (1973), 7-17.

[46]Harper W. Boyd and Sidney J. Levy, "Cigarette Smoking and the Public Interest," *Business Horizons,* Fall 1963, pp. 37-44.

product, a service, advertising, or some other practice is morally offensive? The issues raised by these questions deserve attention, since marketing is both a cause and an effect of conditions within our environment and culture.

More and more, products and services that were once regarded as immoral, taboo, or unmentionable are being marketed vigorously. People can now purchase contraceptives through the mail without the intervention of physicians or pharmacists, and advertisers can freely utilize the traditional media to reach those desiring such products (see Figure 5-3). In many states one can purchase a lottery ticket, bet on a horse race, and play slot machines. Nevada has legalized prostitution, while Florida allows betting on jai alai, dog races, and other sports. Even when thwarted by unavailability or legal restrictions, people will travel great distances or pay high prices to satisfy certain desires. Whether these desires are defined as moral or not, individuals

FIGURE 5-3

A Contemporary Advertisement for Contraceptives

Source: *Daily Northwestern,* February 1974, p. 3.

and organizations are quick to seize opportunities to meet these needs, often developing sophisticated promotional and advertising methods and distribution facilities. In that amorphous and shifting zone between that which is legal and that which is not lies a host of opportunities for conflict and contradictions. The struggle goes on around the virtue or vice of the behaviors involved, with much dialogue aimed at promoting one's position, and especially in the efforts to impose or remove legal restraints.

Those who want to increase the individual's freedom to buy and sell reason that personal freedom is more important than the abuses or ills that he may work on himself. They talk about "victimless crimes," so that individuals should be legally free to be addicted to alcohol, drugs, or gambling; to be suicidal, nonpregnant, or a seller of sexual relations. Assenting to the special role of children and the sensibilities of objectors, these freedoms may be reserved to consenting adults, to privacy where others are not offended, or to given locales where the community values differ from those of society at large (e.g., nudist beaches). Opponents of the permissiveness implied here hark to other values than personal freedom—the inherent cruelty in the killing of animals, the human or spiritual status of a fetus or an embryo, and the damage (physical, emotional, financial) that addicts do to others as well as to themselves.

In summary, this chapter has explored the proposition that conflict in marketing is inherent in the many individual and social values that interact to form the total marketing system. By accumulating examples from several of the points of interaction, the differences among people are shown to operate at various levels of abstraction, to be differences in expression of what they prize, aspire to, will tolerate or accept, despise and seek to destroy. The vitality and force of these expressions are thus not derived from solely economic elements but show what lies behind all ordinary and extraordinary products and services of everyday commercial marketing.

CHAPTER SIX

The Management of
Marketing Conflict

Conflict is by definition inevitable and can never be totally eliminated. It is probably prudent to think of how it is managed, alleviated, moderated, reduced, or perhaps temporarily resolved. As indicated, it can be welcomed as a necessary condition for change and growth, although it is customarily viewed as a problem to be solved. While it is clear that the widespread and often intense character of differences is discouraging, it is also apparent that people are strongly motivated toward doing something constructive about them. The dynamic movement produced by conflict is like the swing of a pendulum in one direction—a countermovement must occur.

It has been noted that conflict has a tendency to escalate, to feed on itself as the parties to it compete, exaggerate and justify, and become committed to the struggle, misperceiving, distorting, or even losing sight of what the conflict is basically or originally about.[1] In many cases this escalation does not occur. That is, each encounter of differences has a life history, for better or worse. The variations are due to general elements and to specific situational events that are conducive to preventing, easing, or—for the while—ending conflicts.

FORCES OPPOSING CONFLICT

These are among the basic forces that either keep conflict from growing or operate to diminish it:

The Urge to Solve Problems.   Considered as an intellectual matter, it seems characteristic of people that when obstacles are encountered, there is a tendency aroused to solve them. It has been suggested that thinking originated in the encounter of obstacles. As Bartlett has stated, thinking has

---

[1]Morton Deutsch, *The Resolution of Conflict* (New Haven, Conn.: Yale University Press, 1973), p. 351.

direction and "it is quite certain that everyday thinking is strongly slanted toward definite decisions." [2] This purposiveness of mental functioning includes such features as appropriateness to the goal, persistence, and searching.[3] The urgency people feel is often more pronounced as the goal or solution becomes clear. This drive toward completion is interpreted as rooted in an inherent need for closure. In itself, problem solving is neutral and can be applied toward negative or positive goals. To the extent that it functions to resolve specific issues for the individual, it helps to reduce subjective conflicts.

Personal Qualities.   Individuals vary in their intellectual capacity to sustain conflict and to bring about harmony. Such qualities as breadth of perspective, mental fatigue, distractibility, acuity of observation, and ability to make distinctions are instrumental in making possible, or interfering with, either a conflict or an amelioration.

Other personal qualities that play a role in determining the degree of integration or disruption that occurs in a given situation include the individual's dependency, optimism, ability to fight, defensiveness, and sensitivity.

Social Aims.   People have a variety of motives that are social in character, which include the desire to cooperate and affiliate, to be like others, or to so integrate differences as to produce unity. Conflict has an affiliative role when the complementarity of debate, sexual intercourse, games, or even boxing is taken as expressing shared aims, or as providing mutual satisfaction. Social, affiliative aims—what Garrett has called "syntality"—express human empathy, an ability to feel with others. Where competition, aggression, and provocation are less prevalent, there is a sense of transcendence, a heightening of social awareness resulting in combined action that is communal rather than individual. Ruth Benedict has called societies of this type high-synergy societies and notes some of the conditions that make high synergy more probable, conditions that distinguish the intimate, commercial, and social marketing activities of the community:

1. Families are not isolated, and involve more people than mother and father in child care.
2. Wealth is distributed widely rather than narrowly.
3. Religious and social forces are benevolent rather than hateful and punishing.[4]

Social analyses of the forces binding people together are extensive, from Plato's *Republic,* allotting society's segments to their just places, to Freud's *Group Psychology and the Analysis of the Ego,* to *The Imperial Animal* of

[2]Frederick Bartlett, *Thinking* (New York: Basic Books, Inc., Publishers, 1958), p. 174.

[3]D. Bindra, *Motivation: A Systematic Reinterpretation* (New York: The Ronald Press Company, 1959).

[4]Ruth Benedict, "Synergy—Patterns of the Good Culture," *Psychology Today,* 4, No. 1 (1970), pp. 53-55, 74, 75, 77. Also in *American Anthropologist,* 72, No. 2 (1970).

Tiger and Fox. The latter two works may be summed up by the sardonic comment of a woman who had just been excluded from a conference being held at an austere men's club: "Latent homosexuality is the glue that holds the business world together."

Basic Processes. Some theories point to the general flow of events as inevitably operating to mitigate conflict. At their core is usually some concept of equilibrium or homeostasis. The events being observed are those of a system in action, pressures of deprivation or wishfulness building up in the individual or group over time, leading to some expressive occurrence that reduces tension through release and gratification. The cycle need not be explosive or highly visible but occurs almost casually in everyday situations where minor conflicts and their dissipation ebb and flow in accustomed rhythms as choices are made and transactions amiably concluded.

Conflicts not so readily managed may continue with variations in intensity as the energy of the participants changes. New conflicts may inflate or shrink old ones, new leadership may point to fresh solutions, and the passage of time may bring a conflict to a natural end as no longer relevant.

Diagnosis and Prescription. A significant approach to marketing conflict and its management involves the logic of diagnosing the reasons for the particular kind of conflict and then seeking the strategy or technique suited to it. When the analysis is oriented to the incompatible personal or social strivings of the individuals, solutions are often forms of *therapy,* usually some strategy for gaining insight or catharsis. Consumers who are unhappy about their consumption of alcohol, fattening foods, or cigaretts may find greater comfort through such treatment.

Behavioral modification through systematic application of rewards and punishments is a controversial approach, especially when it seems severely applied to make prisoners give up marketing in the shadow system. But it is a common and traditional form of managing conflict to use behavioristic methods by reinforcing acceptable acts and seeking to extinguish bad habits by criticism or worse.

EVERYDAY ADAPTATIONS

Several examples will be cited to illustrate various specific ideas about means of conflict management. Because people are commonly motivated to lessen conflict, the fabric of everyday life is continually rent and rewoven as they try to move toward their aims and as they encounter obstacles and make adaptations. In doing so, many actions are relatively spontaneous, an acting out of the assumptions and values underlying or implicit in them. In other cases, people work more self-consciously toward resolutions, exhorting themselves and each other, with the exhortations being barbs in the struggle or balm to the wounds.

Adaptations may be classified as moving in three main directions: toward the self, toward the other, and toward mutual adjustments. All three directions are apt to be operating together, but one may predominate.

Self-oriented methods refer to those adaptations one makes in reducing the conflict from one's own side. They range from just avoiding doing what seems certain to exacerbate the conflict to various other kinds of yielding to the situation. *Self-restraint,* drawing back, cutting down on doing what elicits criticism or attack is one of the most important and obvious mollifying behaviors. In the fall of 1973 it was reported that Japan was resorting to "orderly marketing" arrangements to limit her large export surplus which was arousing resentment in America and Europe. This kind of recognition of criticism by showing self-control is thought to be a useful approach in the public arena to avoid escalating the conflict to an overly dangerous point. In a talk about consumerism, regulation, and advertising, Jock Elliott, chairman of the Ogilvy and Mather advertising agency, pointed out that although criticism of advertising is excessive, it may result in some progress, as Upton Sinclair's exaggerated criticisms of the meat industry had resulted in the first Federal Meat Inspection Act.[5] *Being reasonable* about criticism (Elliott went on reasonably to call for more information before any further federal acts), like so many techniques, is both a way to fight, as it may co-opt the opponent, and a way to ease down on conflict. Not long ago one of Ralph Nader's natural "enemies," the president of the U.S. Chamber of Commerce, said that businessmen should hear Nader out, as he voices "the dissatisfactions and the frustrations that are widespread among American consumers." These are instances of the numerous nonattacking mechanisms along the lines of taking small comfort, watching and waiting, looking for a silver lining, *being civil and optimistic.* A sophisticated but cheerful voice of this sort is Neil Jacoby, who predicts that government and corporations will harmonize their elemental conflicts in the long run.[6] Another variant is *being candid,* admitting to fault from within the criticized group, as Irving Kristol does in an article in the *Wall Street Journal* urging candor on corporations:

> In any democracy, large and powerful organizations which are in business to make a profit will inevitably be regarded—have always been regarded—with distaste and suspicion . . . grossly overstating their earnings . . . sleazy accounting, shrewd accounting technically honest but still misleading accounting. [7]

[5]Jock Elliott, "Another Speech on Consumerism, Regulation and Things That Go Boo in the Night" (Western Region Meeting of the American Association of Advertising Agencies, October 15, 1973).

[6]Neil H. Jacoby, *Corporate Power and Social Responsibility* (New York: The Macmillan Company, 1973).

[7]Irving Kristol, "The Credibility of Corporations," *Wall Street Journal,* January 17, 1974, p. 12.

Many conflicts are resolved when the self-control exercised by one side is acceptable to the other. In a democracy, some form of "voluntary" action is thought more desirable than an externally imposed and policed behavior. The individual then ideally does the "right" thing because his conscience dictates it, because he wants to uphold the values represented by the approved action, rather than because he fears punishment. Often, of course, this self-control is a kind of compromise between sincerity and external force. The *consent decree,* whereby a company denies having been at fault and promises never to do it again, is perhaps a version of such compromise. Another prominent form of such marketing adaptation is the formulation of an industry, association, or professional *code.* Individual members may not agree with the specific values or restraints of the code, but self-regulation by the in-group is recognized as a way of avoiding more trouble from the outside. When the code works, the situation is harmonious for a time, but eventually members of the group test the limits of the code or refuse to abide by it to gain some competitive or express advantage. When enough do this, the code is destroyed and a new one may or may not come into being.

A classic instance was the code adopted in 1930 by the Motion Picture Producers and Distributors of America. The code was ostensibly adhered to voluntarily, and it explicitly stated that "no one is compelled to produce motion pictures in accordance with Code regulations. No attempt is made to force producers to accept the service of the Production Code Administration." Of course, the code had been prepared and initiated with the help of nonproducers: Martin Quigley, editor of the Motion Picture Herald, and the Reverend Daniel A. Lord, S.J., who was described as "a trained moralist with an interest in the theater," but probably some producers and distributors had, in Gilbert Seldes's phrase, "an honest desire to make the movies respectable."

As society's values changed, perhaps in part due to or facilitated by violators of the code, it became obsolete. Society's gradual acceptance of films that show nudity or contain profanity liberated the producers from the code.

The National Association of Broadcasters is currently in the process of making adaptations to the newly perceived needs of children, as described earlier, with the relative freedom of a voluntary code being urged as preferable to rules imposed by the FTC. In a variation on this same theme, Robert Fri of McKinsey and Company recommends that businessmen recognize the new kinds of regulatory agencies coming into being—agencies that do not seek to preserve the structure of a particular industry or merely to control its unsound practices.[8] Rather, newer agencies have as their mission the preservation of the environment, elimination of discrimination in employment, work safety, protection of the consumer, and so forth. Fri's advice to busi-

[8]Robert W. Fri, "Facing Up to Polution Controls," *Harvard Business Review,* March-April 1974, pp. 26-35.

nessmen is to take advantage of the fact that they know the most efficient and economical ways to solve the particular problem the regulator is trying to solve; that is, they know best how they should be regulated, if they will help work it out rather than merely resist.

Other-oriented methods include such overtures as showing good humor, implying that one is not an enemy after all, and showing empathy with the other side—in essence, *inviting compromise.* A classical approach formulated by Charles Osgood is called "graduated reciprocation in tension-reduction," or GRIT.[9] To reverse a vicious circle of escalating conflict, and predicated on a basic desire for relaxation (security, survival), one takes a small step in the hope that it will signal a reduction in threat, a beginning basis for trust or good faith. This approach has been suggested for de-escalating confrontations between great nations. But it also functions in everyday situations, when even a customer's "Wellll . . ." may be taken as a small sign of giving up the conflict, and eliciting a seller's concession in return.

Calling for *general debate* or giving others the chance to air their views— to gain relief of feelings, to feel that all have had a fair chance to contribute— is a means of reducing partisanship. Defending proposed Consumer Protection Agency legislation, Representative Frank Horton tried to introduce this note by pointing out that the bill was prepared after the widest possible discussions with the administration and with business, consumer, and professional groups.

Mutual adjustments are brought about by several major methods. One of the most important is *countervailing power.* When relationships are in balance, the result may be extreme subjective ambivalence in the individual—perhaps most vividly expressed in the immobility of the catatonic schizophrenic frozen between good and evil. In interpersonal, commercial, and social marketing affairs, countervailing power seems valuable in providing mutual checks within conflict situations. Kenneth Galbraith introduced the term to show big business, big government, and big labor checking one another toward beneficial results.

Exchange relationships are governed by *broad understandings and processes* that operate to ameliorate conflict under different circumstances. In an ongoing situation with experience and precedents, there develops a tradition, an ethos, a largely shared outlook. There are common expectations, people know the roles they are supposed to play and how to enact them conventionally. The encounter of differences is viewed as complementary, each party makes suitable statements, and all goes smoothly.

"May I help you?"
"Yes, I am looking for another one of these."
"I have some nice ones right here. The cost is marked on each."
"I'll take this one."
"Is there anything else?"
"No, thank you."

[9]Charles E. Osgood, *An Alternative to War or Surrender* (Urbana: University of Illinois Press, 1962).

In its pure form, the dialogue sounds like an excerpt from a traveler's guide—the point being that if no one deviates from the customary remarks the hope is that the interaction will go well. When the participants conform and obey the expectations of role, of etiquette, *ritualization* is functioning, preventing or minimizing conflict or dictating how it will be handled.[10] Most of the vast flow of marketing events is ordered by ritualization, facilitating the innumerable transactions in which everyone says more or less the right thing.

In a heterogeneous, changing society conflict is active and intense, and ritualization is often disrupted or inadequate. The situation is dynamic, and new understandings have to be arrived at if the change conflict is to remain within some bounds. When the group is unprepared and lacks understanding or transitional mechanism, the conflict may surprise people by its extremity. One classical modern example is the U.S. campus in the sixties where strife and violence erupted without conventional methods at hand to contain it, highlighted by the uncertainty about what role the police should play; another is the sudden appearance of airplane hijacking. Ritualization reflects general agreement on the values that should be implemented. The latter are also called into play in more adaptive situations. Often these values are expressed in precepts, adages, or statements supposed to be taken as obvious guides to proper action: "That government which governs least governs best," "Give the task to the one that will do the best job," "The change will lower morale," "But all the kids have them." In themselves, such assertions may be weapons in the conflict; but when they reflect and elicit the agreement to which they are supposed to refer, they may act to resolve the difference.

Differences are stopped, at least in behavior, when people acquiesce to law. Laws, rules, and regulations may be seen as breathing spells in the conflicts over the issues they govern. They mean that for the while, long or short, some values have won out over others and will hold sway. Much struggle in marketing conflict—perhaps most in a "society of law"—is the struggle to create (prevent) a law or to overturn (protect) one that is on the books. *Legislation* is the way the community keeps ruling on the issues of interest to it. It is based on the kind of agreements made in a representative government where "the majority rules" and the others abide by it. Of course, the process does not always produce results that favor the majority. Special interests constantly lobby for legislation that will improve their positions. An industry may lose ground, from its point of view, on one front while making progress in furthering its goals in another direction, depending on the distribution of power. For instance, the broadcasters have been pressed by some consumer groups and by the FTC, as described earlier, to exercise increasing restraint with regard to children's programming and advertising. The power of these "outside" demands has been steadily increased. In a statement by the FTC

---

[10]Not to be confused with *ritualism* in which blind or stubborn adherence to formula may be used to thwart other people.

staff it was noted that premiums are harmful, confusing, and distracting to children because such devices bear no relation to the attributes or merits of the products being promoted and therefore should not be advertised.

> The National Association of Broadcasters' premium guidelines acknowledge the dangers inherent in the premium device by attempting to limit their use. The staff is of the view, however, that the limitations imposed by these guidelines do not adequately meet the issues posed by TV advertising of premiums to children.[11]

While being forced to retreat by the FTC's recent vigor, the broadcasters appear to be more successful and powerful with the FCC in the fundamental area of licensing law. Andrew Kopkind laments these results:

> The triumphs of the big broadcasters have not completely precluded attempts by small groups of critics and social minorities for reform—or a piece of the action. The "consumer advocacy" of the last two years has affected broadcasting, too. Specifically, it struck in three ways: the assault on the law and process of licensing broadcast outlets; the pressure for "alternative" radio programming; and the proposals for public "access" to television for the display of unconventional opinions.
>
> Now most of the skirmishes, experiments, and litigations in the wars against Big Broadcasting are coming to an end. "Access" has been closed off in many cities by Federal Communications Commission rule and Supreme Court decision. Attempts to expand or experiment with alternative radio broadcasting have been halted or reversed. And any remaining hopes of successful challenges to the broadcast licensing procedure will soon be canceled by coordinated acts of Congress, the courts, and the commission.
>
> •   •   •
>
> The measure (HR 12993) has already swept through the House (379 to 19) and it is now before Pastore's subcommittee, where of course it will be graciously treated. It would extend the duration of licenses from three to five years; establish a performance criterion of "substantial" rather than "superior" service for renewal applicants; eliminate considerations of media concentration and monopoly from license applications or challenges (all pending challenges on the basis of monopoly would also be discarded); and take jurisdiction for FCC matters out of the hands of the consumer-minded District of Columbia Circuit Court of Appeals.
>
> •   •   •
>
> "I'm approaching the end of my rope," a communications lawyer and former FCC staff assistant told me recently. He has spent the last several years waging legal fights for public access to the world of Big Broadcasting. Now, with the court, Congress, and the commission cracking down, he fears the cause of communications advocacy is all but lost. "There's less and less that reform-minded people are able to do to bring diversity to the media, to break it loose. The broadcasters say that with less regulation, they will be free to open up their channels. So we're all supposed to hope for benevolent dictators. As for me, I must say I'm not content to put my hope in CBS to present my viewpoint every so often on "Sixty-Minutes." [12]

[11] Also see proposal to ban advertising of premiums in television commercials directed at children twelve years old and younger, *Federal Register,* July 11, 1974.

[12] Andrew Kopkind, "TV Guide," *New York Review of Books,* August 8, 1974, pp. 33-34.

Ritualization and law are ways of resolving differences that are known as *norm following*.[13] To reach norms that can then prevail for a time, *negotiating or bargaining* may be called upon. Much has been written on this topic, particularly in reference to labor-management relations.[14] Negotiation usually refers to the verbal exchange and verbal agreement aspect of bargaining, while bargaining includes all the activities in which the parties engage to exchange pressures, to elicit concessions, to reach a conclusion. Since bargaining can become synonymous with all exchange interactions aimed at resolving a situation not already governed by norms, the tactics or ploys that people use can be endlessly cataloged to include threats, subtle movement, crying, seeming indifference, apparently giving up, shows of strength, calling on allies, accusations, sweetenings, excusing the greater crime for the lesser (as in plea bargaining), secrecy, and so forth.

At the heart of the bargaining is some notion of hope for an accord; otherwise it would be futile to persist—and even then, some hope against hope. Often, also, there is the belief that a certain basis for the accord exists, consisting of the intersection of how far each party can go and no further, and that the function of the negotiating is one of discovery. The probing to find that point of intersection requires an interplay of greater and lesser values until the critical ones have been revealed or triggered. General value is placed on a result that is considered mutually advantageous, and it is felt that "unconditional surrender" or total defeat are inhumane, and that for the overriding sake of mutual dignity, the stronger antagonist should hold some of his power in abeyance.

When the actors in a conflict are unable to reach an agreement, the intervention of a third party may be used. The role of the third party is in general an interesting one. It is said that three is a crowd, and often the introduction of a third party into a relationship follows a course the participants did not anticipate. The third party may worsen the conflict; sometimes the original conflict disappears as the disputants join each other and turn against the third party. Third parties are traditionally introduced into situations where an actor feels unable to pursue his aims on his own or to cope with the obstacles that arise in encountering others. The third party becomes a *representative* of the buyer, the seller, or sometimes ambiguously of both, as with matchmakers, brokers, interior decorators. Another important role of the third party is to act as *judge*. In this case, the third party is given the power to decide the issue, to terminate the conflict by his fiat. In intimate marketing conflicts a judge may decide on the allocation of resources among family members, who gives and who gets what, decisions that radiate naturally into decisions about commercial marketing actions. The judge adjudicates commercial disputes over contracts, credit arrangements, collections, variously

[13]Dean G. Pruitt, "Methods for Resolving Differences of Interest," *Journal of Social Issues,* 28, No. 1 (1972), 133-54.

[14]R. E. Walton and R. B. McKersie, *A Behavioral Theory of Labor Negotiations* (New York: McGraw-Hill Book Company, 1965).

protecting the interests of buyers, sellers, or some concept of what is socially desirable. An informal version of this role is enacted by the manager or supervisor who is brought in by the irate customer who hopes that his higher authority and understanding will overrule the mistaken, stubborn, or menial salesman.

John P. Spiegel has described several third-party interveners: the advocate, the conciliator, the mediator, the arbitrator, and the research evaluator. [15] The *advocate* is a particular kind of representative. He may be partisan by conviction, coming in as an outside organizer, not of the group but with it in its aims, perhaps advising actions to take. In a more stylized way, a lawyer plays this role, arguing on behalf of his client, usually with less personal commitment to the issue, and abiding by the rules of resolving conflict observed in the court. The *conciliator* tends to represent the interests of both sides, seeking to cool the passions, perhaps helping the combatants to gain insight into their motives, to gain distance, to hold off from precipitous action. The *mediator* (conceivably the same person) may then be in a position to help the parties recognize their mutual interests or to reach a mutually satisfactory settlement.

The *arbitrator* may be like a judge who has the authority to impose a settlement, something exhausted battlers may welcome and be glad to have as someone else to blame. Some with the title of arbitrator are only mediators or consultants, the arbitration not being binding. Arbitration is compulsory in many industrial situations, determining the conditions under which labor will be marketed. The relief with which this type of third-party intervention is welcomed is shown in the growth of voluntary arbitration, although there is also frequent dispute as to which issues are arbitrable. The American Arbitration Association promotes its services to the community: its division, the National Center for Dispute Settlement, advertised in *Business Week,* July 21, 1973, that conflict was healthy but could get out of hand. It boasts of having resolved hundreds of disputes and offers a quick, fair, and inexpensive service.

When the mutuality established in relationships, whether through the high-synergy socialization process or through the various mechanisms mentioned above, is considerable, the participants respond to each other affirmatively, trying to adapt to the needs being expressed by each other. By following this norm of mutual responsiveness (mutual backscratching), it is often possible to obviate negotiation, bargaining, escalation of conflict, and so forth.[16] Much rhetoric is oriented toward persuading sides in a conflict toward this willingness.

This approach is notable in contemporary attempts by businessmen to adapt themselves and their peers to the consumerism movement. A certain

---

[15]John P. Spiegel, "The Social Role of Antagonists and Third-Party Interveners in Violent Confrontations," *International Journal of Group Tensions,* 3, Nos. 1-2 (1973), 142-51.

[16]Pruitt, *op. cit.,* p. 147.

probing process goes on in which certainty is sought concerning the strength and persistence of the need. Not uncommonly, people are willing to do things for someone else when it becomes apparent that the other person feels strongly about the matter: "Well, if it's *that* important to you." In the commercial marketing sphere, polls are taken, and market researches are carried out in depth to learn if the consumers really do care, if consumerism is here to stay. Consumerism vaguely covers all sorts of complaints—misleading advertising, labeling, warranties, problems with nutrition, appliance repair, television for being television, pollution, energy crisis. The response to consumerism takes specific forms—FTC regulations, legislation oriented to consumer protection, debate over whether regulatory agencies can avoid domination by their client industries—and positive response is summed up in the idea of social responsibility. When adoption of social responsibility is urged on members of the business community by other members, it is a way of saying that "we and the consumer need each other, we love each other, we identify with each other, their needs are our needs." If so, the supposed singular centrality of the profit motive is inadequate and fails to recognize the larger aims to which all should be devoted. G. Robert Truex of the Bank of America, writing to the editors of *Fortune* magazine, says:

> We are in the midst of a major readjustment of values in this country. Uncontrolled growth is being seriously and effectively challenged. Demands for protection of the environment, for product quality and safety, for promotional integrity, for affirmative action employment, and for job enrichment are not just passing fads. They are the realities of today's business milieu. [17]

His is one such voice among many pointing out that the conflict between consumers and business is not or should not be a real one, that social and corporate responsibility is an essential response and an expression of corporate interest.

To some, giving positive response to other people implies yielding up some degree of autonomy, freedom of action. The radical free enterpriser wants no restraints on his conduct of business; the radical intimate marketer wants no family ties to inhibit him; the pirate wants to pay no price. But in the largest sense, conflict is resolved when something is yielded for the sake of social living. To agree to cooperate is to establish an organization and to agree to forgo some actions. Such agreement exists at many levels in society, but there is a long way to go. The problem is universal, and especially noticeable on the international scene. In March 1973 in Amsterdam, at the Europe-America Conference, Max Kohnstamm, director of the European Community Institute for University Studies, said, "What is lacking is the willingness of nations to surrender some of their sovereignty to a joint cause."

---

[17]G. Robert Truex, Jr., "Corporate Responsibility," *Fortune.* August 1973, p. 27.

Epilogue

The thrust of this volume has been to discuss the nature of marketing from some less customary or traditional points of view. The goal was to explore basic ideas concerning the role of marketing in the society as a general process, and as exemplified in numerous specific contexts. Building on a sequence of steps, the argument is simply this:

1. Marketing is the interaction of those who want something (anything) and those who provide something (anything).

2. To conceptualize the various contents and relationships in this root view of marketing, it is recognized that marketing phenomena are not only economic but are manifestations of types of social systems. Thus marketing is susceptible to study through the concepts and methods of the behavioral sciences.

3. Conversely, it is recognized that social systems are not only behavioral phenomena but are manifestations of types of marketing. This is the "broadening" notion of marketing.

4. Therefore, among other viewpoints for analysis, all interactions can be interpreted as marketing situations.

5. In making such analysis and interpretation, various spheres can be discriminated, here described as intimate marketing, commercial marketing, and social marketing.

6. In all marketing situations, there is an encounter of differences—that is, a conflict in aims, resources, intensity, interest, kinds of people involved, means employed, and so forth.

7. The possibilities of conflict are infinitely various, and can be examined for their subjective form and content, in transactions between and among people and groups, in relation to personal, economic, and social nexuses.

8. Specific marketing conflicts are enjoyed, diminished, terminated, and transformed through various processes, usually interpreted as constructive.

The implications of this argument may be taken in several directions. As a participator in the contention of views about marketing, this volume defends marketing against the synecdochic criticism it receives because some aspects of it are found unattractive. Marketing is defended as an inevitable process

in which even its critics are seen as within it, necessarily engaged in marketing their views and pleading that marketing take certain preferred forms.

Such a perspective on marketing is in a sense a large hypothesis—or definition—asserting that behind every marketing act of giving or getting lie all
the requirements of being an actor in the society and a member of its diverse
subgroups, expressing the attendant personal and social values of the particular system.

From a research point of view, many issues are raised for study. Can the
perspective offered here affect the vantage point of marketing scholars? As
mentioned earlier, many of them (most?) have tended to study from somewhat "closer in" the commercial marketing system, therefore studying marketing processes that are aimed at enhancing the traditional efforts of marketing managers to know their markets in order to maximize their profits,
making most marketing literature less analytic than it is prescriptive. One
always has some value position, of course, but it may be useful to marketing
students to back off somewhat for greater detachment, to see the commercial
marketing process as it is embedded in the larger marketing processes of the
society. For social scientists, who are frequently inclined to take an anti-
marketing position, intellectual benefit may be drawn from substituting
analytic perspectives for some moral judgments, in the hope of long-run
improvement of the latter.

If it is assumed that in a democratic society it is advantageous to increase
the possibilities for freedom of choice and self-expression, the encourage-
ment of differences is supported. Then it seems good that the marketing
process is not a set thing, but that *conflict is its core dynamism,* one leading
to constant modification, diversity, and avoidance of an overly oppressive
"cake of custom." Similarly, one hopes for sufficient synergism in the
society, and for enough of the mechanisms of ritualization and constructive
adaptation, of goodwill and consonance, as we work toward the Utilitarians'
dream of the greatest good for the greatest number, even if this dream is a
paradox along the lines of unendurable pleasure indefinitely prolonged.

Index